Praise for Esa Aldegheri's *Fr*

"In her account of an epic _____ ly scaled expedition into the trauma that was the recent pandemic, Esa Aldegheri opens the book on the most elemental aspects of being alive: tested by trials, gripped by the varieties of love, and crossing borders both internal and drawn on the map."
—Melissa Holbrook Pierson

"A thought-provoking and elegiac journey through a lost world on a second-hand motorbike, the past, present and life itself."
—Chitra Ramaswamy

"A very readable tale of adventure, motherhood and the ties that bind. Honest and perceptive, *Free to Go* perfectly captures the whole tricky business of being a free-spirited woman at large in the world." —Lois Pryce

"An exhilarating story of freedom and constraint, told with a confident and unwavering verve. This is a journey driven by boundless curiosity, and by the desire for connection – across borders, across languages, across time." —Malachy Tallack

THERE SHE GOES

NEW TRAVEL WRITING BY WOMEN

EDITED BY ESA ALDEGHERI

Saraband

Published by Saraband,
3 Clairmont Gardens,
Glasgow, G3 7LW

www.saraband.net

ISBN: 9781916812093

Printed and bound in Great Britain by Clays Ltd, Elcograf S.p.A.

10   9   8   7   6   5   4   3   2   1

GPSR: There are no known safety hazards associated with this product.

We are grateful to Creative Scotland and the National Lottery Fund
for financial support enabling the creation of this book.

LOTTERY FUNDED

For readers everywhere who are interested in stories about women moving in a world we all share

CONTENTS

INTRODUCTION

There She Goes is inspired by a great sisterhood of women who, over the years, have shared their travel stories with me in cafés, on walks, over drinks, in kitchens, in corners of time snatched between the commitments of life and caring. Tales of walking alone in a city at night. Periods arriving in the least convenient places. Travelling to get an abortion, or life-saving healthcare, or transformative surgery. Hot flushes in an overcrowded train. Breastfeeding on pilgrim trails, in cafés, in car parks, to disapproval or support. Being welcomed into kitchens where men are not allowed. Being the only dark-skinned or light-skinned woman around. Navigating the world as a new mother. Steering through deep, incapacitating pain and loss. Moving through a supermarket in a new country trying to find what your body needs, everything foreign, everything strange.

These stories are met by laughs, gasps, horrified silence, nods of recognition – and always prompt a cascade of other tales in response. They are remarkable for their everyday nature, rooted in the common experience of moving through the world as a woman; they are also as various as the shifting kaleidoscope of women's lives, bodies and choices. And yet, they are largely absent from the canon of 'real', published travel writing.

In recent efforts to reclaim this historically male-dominated genre, many anthologies of women's travels and travel writing have featured women engaged in brave, bold achievements, against the odds or ahead of their time. Their stories are often shaped by the language of conquest, of fighting against death and fear, of extreme endurance outdoors in places that are 'the ends of the earth' or 'the middle of nowhere'. Look, they say, women too have been and can be just as bold, just as tough, brave, wild, strong … as men.

Yes, we know that to be true. And yes, certainly, we still need to push against the voices which continue to restrict what women can and can't do. But why do we still need to be defined by the patriarchal parameters of heroic achievement which have so long dominated travel writing? Do women really need to run across deserts, kayak the coast of Siberia or almost die in the jungle for their travel writing to be published? Where are our other stories, the ones so often shared verbally, so vivid with the everyday reality of what happens when women move through the world in their brave, scared, messy bodies? This anthology is one answer to these questions; in turn, it seeks to question categories which limit what women should and should not be, or write. Its title is a response, of sorts, to a particularly disappointing man who once – years ago, as I shared my thoughts with a group of friends in the pub – sighed and said, "There she goes. On about women and 'real travel writing', again."

There She Goes features seventeen exceptionally talented wordsmiths; women who write from a wide range of ages, backgrounds, bodies and experiences. All responded with enthusiasm when invited to be part of this anthology; many added the interesting caveat of not feeling they were a 'real travel writer'. I thought of Jan Morris, and how she preferred to consider herself as a writer who travelled, rather than a travel writer. All the contributors to this anthology are writers who travel, a fine company whose words celebrate the grit, courage, adventure and determination of women moving through the world in a variety of ways: with babies, with loss and grief and gladness, with periods, with the wisdom of age, with magic and humour, with bodies that are unwell or seen as foreign and Other.

INTRODUCTION

Gathering this book into being has been a joy. As with all the best adventures, I had no idea what would happen when it began to take shape. I have delighted in watching how the writers, independently from each other, crafted stories that connect with each other through shared themes, like paths interweaving.

Many authors explore what it means to leave home, to return home, to stay at home. Roxani Krystalli goes back to Greece – the home she left before travelling a great deal and then making her new home in Scotland. She takes us on a journey through memory, language and belonging, discovering solitude and joy and 'the hope that, by experiencing the world otherwise, we may feel, or think, or dream differently, even for a minute'. Leena Rustom Nammari shares her experience of crossing the El-Jisir bridge – the only official border crossing between the West Bank and Jordan – as a Palestinian travelling away from her homeland. Here, language and belonging are linked to practices of apartheid, but also to expressions of solidarity and resistance. Leena's journey shows how the injustices of Israel's occupation are made manifest through travel restrictions which severely limit the right of Palestinian people to leave or return to their homeland.

In contrast, Linda Cracknell is free to travel across many borders on her journey by train from her home in Scotland to a writing retreat in Morocco. Linda traces the transformation in perspective that this journey brings her as she moves between landscapes, languages and food traditions. She shifts from anxiety about travel logistics to acceptance, reflecting on how travelling changes as we go through different life phases. Amanda Thomson, too, considers how travel has formed and changed the way she lives in the world, linking her own experiences to the inspiring travels of her mother. She weaves a meditation on travel, memory, belonging, and what it means to move through the world as a Black woman with a female partner. Amanda also asks, in the light of all her travels, what it means to stay. This question is approached from a different angle by Sarah Thomas, in her essay 'Stay at Home'. Sarah describes her experience of moving towards stillness and deep connection with the natural world near her home in Dumfries and Galloway during Covid-19 lockdowns. When her house becomes a place of fear due to a threatening male neighbour, Sarah spends more and more time roaming the woods nearby and finds a safe haven near a heronry, by the river estuary.

The natural world as a place of beauty, solace and discovery is a theme central to the writing of other authors. Leonie Charlton traces a trip made with a dear travelling companion, by horse and on foot, in the Scottish Highlands, and shows how words can inform and transform how we travel across landscapes. In many ways, Leonie's trek is a pilgrimage through land and languages to find out what it means to be truly awake, wherever we are. Pilgrimage, historically, was one of the few legitimate ways in which women could travel long distances; Claire Askew shares a modern account of pilgrimage in her story of going to Salem, Massachusetts, to honour and mourn the people who were murdered during the Salem Witch Trials. She also charts her own inner journey of faith and worship to find out where a Christian witch can go to make herself a sacred space and rejoice in our beautiful world. Anna Fleming takes us on an expedition-pilgrimage up Mont Blanc, a place of sacred beauty which is increasingly vulnerable to climate change. It is also a place where the stories and needs of women's bodies have long been sidelined, as Anna finds out when she arrives in a mountain refuge full of men and – of course – her period starts. She challenges heroic narratives of mountaineering conquest by writing of physical strength alongside vulnerability.

4

INTRODUCTION

Narratives related to endurance and quest develop along different paths in this anthology. In 'Rewriting the Hero's Journey', Lee Craigie and some friends upend the competitive parameters of an off-road bike race in the Highlands of Scotland. They complete the race fast and well while prioritising care of themselves, each other and the landscapes they race through; they reject narratives which suggest that truly heroic races are the ones featuring the most pain or aggression. Marjorie Lotfi's story explores care, courage and endurance in the context of being a busy mother of four children who always puts herself last. Through sea swimming and marathon training, Marjorie realises her needs and her limits, and discovers just how far her body can go; in doing so, she finds a sense of safety and of homecoming. A different kind of homecoming is charted by Alice Tarbuck, who tells how the domestic rituals of picking and preserving apples help her move through grieving for her beloved Grandmother. Alice's is a quest which does not need vast horizons or feats of physical endurance; rather, it navigates memory and intergenerational connections, love and loss, moving through the seasons of the external world as well as through inner seasons of healing.

Motherhood, mothers and grandmothers appear often in the pages of *There She Goes*. In 'From Our Own Correspondent', Jemma Neville shares travel logs from the strange, terrifying and wonderful land that is new motherhood. She interweaves her own diary – written following the birth of her twins, which happened not long after her firstborn baby died – with the diary her own Grandma wrote as a new mother, decades before. Jemma charts days when getting out of the house is an epic achievement, when the weight of loss is carried alongside the joy of new life. Kerri ní Dochartaigh describes her own unexpected matrescence journey during times of Covid lockdown and the transformative love she experiences, as well as the wilderness of perinatal depression.

Kerri traces her path of recovery – from feeling lost and unable to make her way through a world she can no longer read, to discovering a garden of timeless beauty where she finds unforeseen mothering and a new sense of peace.

Journeys through pain and loss towards healing are among the most ancient and widespread of human travel tales. Here, those stories are related to women and their bodies. Roseanne Watt writes of living with the chronic pain of endometriosis and asks – what do you do in a body that can't travel? She searches for answers by navigating mythology, medical appointments, home-leaving, home-return and family lore handed down by generations of women. The Shaetlan[1] language, Roseanne's midder[2] tongue, shows her a way through the body's wilderness – a way to turn her thoughts towards life, whatever that might mean to her. Languages and translations are threads running through Alison Phipps' story of experiencing the loss of a child while travelling in Germany. Alison writes about carrying this fragmenting, echoing pain across time and landscapes; finding connection with Sappho's poetry, which arrives to us in translated fragments; and finding some solace not through dry prose or medical reports, but in the natural world and the vivid imagery of poetry and dreams.

We travel to Italy with Janette Ayachi, who falls in love with a passionate Italian man and his country. She becomes a mother – but must then tread a difficult path of truth-finding and self-realisation. Navigating some of motherhood's most difficult choices and sacrifices, Janette has to extricate herself from a family situation which becomes oppressive and harmful. With Margaret Elphinstone we journey through time, as well as through place, as she shares wisdom from a lifetime of travel and writing. She

1   Shetland

2   mother

shows us how time circles like the returning waves that 'swell, fall, crash, swirl' and mark her journeys as a writer, as a woman, as a mother. Margaret takes us across seas and centuries, through stories and memories, to Iceland and Faroe, between the islands of Scotland. With her, we see how each one of our journeys is a tiny drop in an ocean of stories that stretches far beyond our individual lives.

In many ways this book, too, is just a wee drop in a wider conversation about stories which until now have rarely been included in the printed canon of 'travel writing'. I know that I would have loved to read such a book myself as I first planned my own travels through the world as a young woman. But *There She Goes* is not a book only for women; it is for all those people who are interested in a broader conversation about bodies moving in a world we all share, about whose stories are 'important', and whose experiences are worthy of printing and reading and sharing. In times where fear and conflict seem increasingly prevalent, it is a gift of courage and celebration – a book of travel stories where places are made new through the words on the page.

Esa Aldegheri

TRAVELLING HOME FROM HOME

Roxani Krystalli

I.

My childhood memories of travel are intensely peopled. Travelling often involved the same cast of characters as our home life, but it came with the promise – the hope, the illusion – of these people and relationships feeling different if we all slept a short distance from home. Any journey started with deep cleaning our home from top to bottom. It did not matter that the house was already clean, or that we would have to clean again on our return to chase away the dust that had accumulated in our absence. Every Greek woman in my lineage was raised with the fear that Something might happen while we were away. The imagined Something was inevitably catastrophic (an accident, a burglary, a death), and it would invariably mean that a friend, a neighbour, or, worse, a stranger may have to enter our home without our being there. In this story, the dignity of the family depended on the cleanliness of our home.

The prospect of travel magnified the points of tension baked into our daily lives. There were cleaning fights and packing fights and money fights and fights about how to load the car, and there was always a threat that if Someone did not get their attitude together, my mother would put the car keys down and we would go nowhere. But somehow, we managed to squeeze

8

an assortment of aunts, cousins, and neighbours into cars unfit to carry this load, and we'd be away to the seaside peninsula of Halkidiki.

The children would be reminded in a stern tone not to make a mess of the car and the adults would argue about whether it was acceptable to smoke on the way. "For heaven's sake," one parent would admonish the other, "it is only an hour and a half away," all the while rolling down their own window in preparation for lighting up. We would arrive three hours later, sweaty thighs sticking to the seats, crushed crisps underfoot, with a car fight under our belts and the smell of plastic beach paraphernalia emanating from the boot.

The affectionate quarrelling travelled with us, as did a relentless sense of being observed. Everyone's eating habits, sleeping preferences, manner of dress, and leisure activities would be scrutinised, commented upon, and tallied. How many ice creams Eleni had, how far Konstantinos swam, how many times Mary returned to the buffet quickly turned into a joke or a criticism. Over meals lasting hours, we would recount previous holidays at the same spot, the memory of them mutating with each retelling.

We couldn't be with each other, we couldn't be without each other, we couldn't imagine another way to be. I scan my memories, trying to discern whether someone resembling who I am now had been part of those scenes and had gone unnoticed. Had there been a woman reading happily alone on her beach chair, right beside the raucous families of Greeks having their fifth argument of the day about sun cream? Was there a human somewhere enjoying a sunset drink in their own company? A solitary walk? A table for one? And how might my experience of leisure, of place and travel, of self and home have been different had I been aware of the pleasures of solitude?

II.

The Greek language, I was told as a child, has more words in it than any other. This statement belongs in the realm of national mythologies – part true, mostly invented, and wholly imprinted in memory. I feel most foreign when I search for a word in my mother tongue and cannot find it. It is a foreignness born not in relation to a home or a language, but one that manifests as an estrangement from self.

The words I most seem to lack in Greek are ones that separate the self from the world. I never heard phrases like "alone time" or "solo travel" or even "boundaries" during my childhood. Greek, of course, has words for solitude and for the boundaries that demarcate one house from another, but the contemporary versions of these concepts – the kind seen on Instagram posts or heard on podcasts about how to deal with your family – only entered my vocabulary in my adopted languages. My Greek, meanwhile, remained peopled.

Growing up in Thessaloniki in the 1980s and 1990s, there was no word for the food that gets delivered to one's door in steaming containers. We would eat food we cooked at home, or we would gather at a tavern, our elbows noisily scratching the layer of paper that hid the plastic tablecloths underneath. We ate mostly Greek food – which, to us, was simply 'food' – and we ate it around the table with each other. There were exceptions to this rule, and they shone brightly on account of their exceptionality: a souvlaki eaten standing on a street corner with friends at the end of a night out, a pizza at home during the Champions League games, which was an occasion even for the non-football fans in the family.

As international cuisines became more popular in Greece and the way we ate started to change, we had to import language from English to describe our new way of living. The now commonly used Greek word for food delivery is … 'delivery,' albeit inflected with a Greek accent. The person who brings the food to one's door is called 'deliveras.' A new way of relating to people, food, and time has entered our vernacular without disguising its foreignness.

So it was with 'solo travel' too. The Greek language of my childhood had no terms to readily describe experiencing the world alone. It was through English-language magazines and travel books and blogs that I learned about the mythical 'solo female traveller.' In my mother tongue, both language and modes of living were oriented towards togetherness. This is not to say that all this time spent in the company of others was 'quality time' (another term not seamlessly translatable into Greek). As any Greek teenager who has sat through the enforced togetherness of a very mandatory Sunday lunch of oven roasted chicken with potatoes will recall, shared time was not always companionable, memorable, or even joyful. It was, however, the norm. A person moving through the world alone defied articulation.

III.

In the summer of 2021, I returned home to Greece from my now home in Scotland. Home-from-home is the kind of travel that shuffles internal compasses, rendering it difficult to distinguish 'here' from 'there'; where I live from where I am visiting.

Greeks take pride in hospitality. The guest is, as we say, 'king.' We will fill plates with food, and fill them again, and eye them watchfully until our guests beg for mercy. We will give up our beds for visitors so they can rest well, even if it means we won't. We will put out the good towels and good sheets and good soap – the kind nobody who lives in the house year-round is allowed to use in the absence of a visitor. We will point out antiquities and light, we'll raise glasses and turn our faces to the sun, we'll repeat a chorus of 'σαν στο σπίτι σου' – treat this place like your home. We will do all this with heart, with the kind of committed sincerity that allows a guest to truly exhale, to imagine living there as if it *were* their home, as if we were their people.

In the twenty years I have now lived away from my home in Thessaloniki, I have found it a curiously difficult place to be a guest myself. The hospitality guests enjoy requires foreignness, whereas having become foreign to my home of origin comes with disorientation. By choosing to move away from Greece, I have scrambled my sense of belonging, muddied my own legibility. On each return, I must invent a place for myself anew.

Landing in Thessaloniki again requires the curiosity of reacquaintance. I observe this return as an anthropologist, equipped with the tools of my trade. When it comes to homes and returns, it is easier sometimes to be a professional and a traveller than an immigrant or a daughter. An anthropological eye remains attuned to novelty, open to surprise. Meanwhile, the nostalgia that underpins my own sight is looking for confirmation of my memories.

The place to which I have returned is less peopled than my recollections of it. Nearly every elder who featured in the reminiscences of childhood journeys has now died. Strangers address me formally, with the tone reserved for grown women, «κυρία» (kyria), instead of «δεσποινίς» (despoinis). Every time I am greeted as 'Mrs Krystalli' in Greek, I look behind me, expecting to see my mother.

I am, however, alone by necessity, grief, and choice alike. The complex rules governing travel during this phase of the Covid-19 pandemic make it difficult for others to accompany me. Beyond the logistics, I have a sense that these home-from-home returns may benefit from solitude, from experiencing a place without having to articulate or translate it to others.

I arrive in Greece with a desire to overhear conversation, to discern what the current slang is, to whisper it to myself in the hope of hauling my own Greek to the present. I want to marvel at the women of Thessaloniki who adorn themselves (ourselves?) in a cascade of cosmetics and fabrics and hairstyles, even just to take the bins out. I want to find the pronouns that fit: am I part of the 'we' that does the adorning, or the 'they' who marvel from a distance? I want to inhale the cigarette smoke from the strangers at the next table over and have the olfactory annoyance ground me in place and time. I do not wish to narrate, to tell stories of other selves in other homes, or other lands. I just want to be alone in the company of others and to slowly imagine – partly from memory, partly through reinvention – a new way of being here.

As I inhabit this solitude, I become more aware of what marks me out as a stranger to this home. Standing back from the doors of the bus, I wait for others to disembark before I board. I feel the wave of passengers standing behind me pushing me impatiently forward. It is others' bodies against mine that remind me that 'there' we may queue, but here – here we mob! Holding myself separate from others, even in a gesture of respectful distance, singles me out as foreign to this place.

It is my solitude that most sets me apart. One of the earliest modes of friendship I learned by observing my parents in Greece was the 'errand friend,' the patient human who comes along to the tax authority to stand next to the person whose errand it is in a hybrid mob-queue. The errand friend comes along to the doctor, to the ID office and the department of motor vehicles, to the bank, to the shops to argue with the sales assistant about exchanging one item for another after losing the receipt. She – and it usually is a 'she' – has patience, a sense of humour, stories to tell. Her sense of indignation is at the ready, immediately deployable if someone dares to try slipping in ahead of us.

It is a dual conviction that animates these friendships: Greek bureaucracy produces too much loneliness to navigate alone, and friendship is too important to wait until one is free from bureaucracy.

In the summer of 2021, at the tax authority, at the registry of births and deaths, at the electricity company, I stand alone. My body may have slowly remembered to board buses decisively, but it has forgotten temperature regulation. Scotland quietened my sweat glands, such that when I am dipped back into the forty-degree heat (104°F) of Greece in July, I wilt. Sweaty solitude becomes its own marker of un-belonging.

In this state, I make most sense to fellow Greeks when they can imagine me as travelling for work. It all fits then: I speak Greek, I know how to be here, when to nudge or nag, when to smile and when to sigh – but I don't have people. Our professional selves are less startling to others when alone in the world. We come to expect solitude – loneliness, alienation even – in the domain of work. My compatriots, however, still struggle to imagine solitude in the universe of family and home, in the eyes of the state, in the realm of leisure, or as an outflow of choice.

Friends try to rescue me from myself. Yet, I stubbornly hold on to my pocket of 'alone time,' even if I still have no language for it in my mother tongue. Slowly, each morning, a ritual begins to take shape. I arrive in Aristotelous Square while the pavements are still slippery from the day's cleaning, and choose a café – any café, a different one each day. In this square I learned to ride a bicycle and tried my first corn on the cob, kernels wedged between the braces on my teeth. I had fed the pigeons here as a child, and I'd walked with feigned confidence past the bars as a teenager, wondering if others could tell I was wearing lip gloss. Nearly everything has changed, but on a clear day, Mt Olympus is still visible across the Thermaic gulf.

From a nearby table, I can hear dice rolling on a backgammon board. Though I tend to bring a book, headphones, and sunglasses, I mostly just sit here, listen, and watch, with eyes, ears and heart unshielded. If I allow for openness, a contentment settles in, and a kind of joy too. It is a joy born from porousness to the world.

A waiter appears to take my coffee order. Every day, without fail, a different waiter sets down two glasses of water. "It's just me," I always say, but they leave the second glass anyway. "Just in case," the waiters comment consistently. In case of what? In case of solitude, break the glass.

IV.

July 2021 in Thessaloniki. Same heatwave, different table. The reliable two glasses of water. I am, as I have been all month, the only person sitting alone. I have travelled a long way from my childhood, and so has my homeland, but we have found a way to recognise each other.

I recognise, too, the Greeks at the surrounding tables. We are strangers to each other, but we are bound by the familiar rituals of togetherness. "You ate nothing," one woman complains theatrically to another, "nothing at all!" Everyone involved, including the accidental spectators, knows that is not strictly true, but we also know that this kind of overbearing watchfulness is how Greeks express care.

The turnover rate of the tables is slow. There is no quick sit-down coffee here, no earnestly fast food. I catch snippets of conversation, peppered with questions and reactions, delivered with conviction and care. "No, it's not right. It's a broken state we live in!" "Ach, friend. Your mum will come around." "Women, man! I just don't understand them." Many of the exclamations defy translation, and ought perhaps to remain untranslated. They are offered in intimate gatherings among people fluent in them, not for broader audiences looking in. In every drawn-out consonant, in every fierce nod of the head lies the affirmation of friendship.

Friends come and go, kissing each other on the cheeks, hugging, holding one another at an arm's distance apart to praise an outfit. Are those new earrings? What perfume is that – it smells amazing! I like your trainers, friend. Did you swim this weekend? You have sun on your face. Friendship here is a volley of noticing, holding on to beauty and passing it back and forth. This kind of exuberant affection is not reserved for special occasions, for birthdays or for a *really* nice outfit. Like the nagging and the food pushing, the whining and the gossip, it is woven into the dailiness of life.

This is what the children who crushed crisps onto the floor of the car on the way to Halkidiki have now aged into. This is what our now dead elders used to be like. There is more space now for other ways of being here and there are even, dare I say, fewer smokers. Homes can freeze in memory, and nostalgic immigrants sometimes make for inattentive noticers when we return home. In looking for the flavours, scents, bad behaviours and affectionate habits we recognise, we can miss the ways in which people and place have shed layers in favour of new ways of being.

The solitude I relish contains a softness within it, a permeability to the world that remains open to the possibility of encounter. Here I am, in a place that is familiar and new, home and not home, in a chorus of ghosts and benevolent hauntings. Between the care and the light, the frustration and the joy, here I am, alone but accompanied.

V.

I realise with time that it is not merely a woman's solitude that others find jarring; it is the contentment of that solitude. It is solitude as a settled state, a way of being at ease, at peace. For me, too, the pleasures of solitude – on the road, at home, or between homes – have had to be acquired and learned.

These pleasures exist in a chorus of other feelings. They sit alongside the knowledge that travelling alone means all your time and desires are your own, but so are the frustrations and inconveniences. Pleasures unfold alongside the demands of a fitful body that has its own aches and needs, and beside the caregiving requirements that do not evaporate when one is no longer in their physical proximity. I am intimately aware of this alongside-ness, of living in a world that requires holding multiple truths in one embrace. *And* I wish, for a moment, to celebrate pleasure and contentment and joy in their own light, to speak of joy without caveat, without qualification, of pleasure without apology. I wish to treat 'there she goes' in the spirit of possibility, rather than apprehension, rather than allowing for joy only when we narrate it alongside what aches, demands, and lacks.

It is possibility that sets us out on the road in the first place: the hope that, by experiencing the world otherwise, we may feel, or think, or dream differently, even for a minute. Whether I am travelling for work or pleasure, for anthropological research or to navigate a complicated return home-from-home, a moment I always relish is the one before the first meal at my destination. When I have taken a seat, preferably at the counter, or at a table facing out towards the world, and a menu lands in front of me, my heart is more willing to say yes.

Yes to the exhilaration of novelty, the contentment of the just-right breeze on a linen dress.

Yes to the first walk anywhere, and to the first bench, when everything still lies ahead.

Yes to the serendipity of dappled sunlight through trees and the glimmer of light on water.

Yes to the joy of the last bite of portokalopita, phyllo soaked in honeyed orange syrup.

Yes to the stories we tell seatmates on a bus or a plane, knowing that some truths roll more easily off the tongue in the company of strangers.

Yes to "I am heartbroken," "I have been ill," "I am on the cusp of something," "I am grieving," "I am in love," and to the words that gain a different power when uttered in an unfamiliar place.

Yes to how our own voice surprises us on a quiet day at its first utterance.

Yes to how old selves, old homes, old dreams come to visit in the quiet, and memories shift shapes when bathed in new light.

Yes to the exuberance of an opening, to seeing new art, hearing a new tune, relishing a new flavour.

Yes to how we carry people with us, to the loved ones each flick of paint, scent, bite, and slant of light brings to mind.

Yes to two glasses of water, even if I will only need one. I will drink out of both.

DISPATCHES FROM A ROAD LESS TRAVELLED

Crossing El-Jisir (The Bridge)
With Usama and Saddam

Leena Rustom Nammari

It is ten in the morning. Usama Abdo picks me up in his brand new white and very clean Hyundai, in Beit Hanina, Al-Quds (Jerusalem). Since he is an older, kind-eyed gentleman, he is an Ammo (Uncle) to me. He deserves my respect, as he is the age I think of an ammo, mid- to-late sixties.

Ammo Usama will be taking me to El-Jisir (The Bridge).

After our hugs and kisses, my dad stands to the side of the Hyundai, holding back his tears, and I climb in, holding back mine. It is Dad who usually takes me to my departure points. It is he who usually takes me to the dreaded Ben Gurion Airport, or, as some of us still call it, Matar-el-Lydd (El-Lydd Airport). But in these unprecedented and extraordinary times, on October 31st, 2023, there is really no other option, neither for the airlines nor for us Palestinians, to be travelling through hostile lands.

So, I am crossing El-Jisir. El-Jisir's full name is Jisir El-Malik Hussein, or the King Hussein Bridge, for Palestinians, and the Allenby Bridge for the Israelis and others. Allenby is a colonial name, named after a British General after the establishment of the British Mandate of 1918. We just call it El-Jisir. People would cross El-Jisir for a day trip before 1967, when Israel occupied the rest of

Palestine – the West Bank and the Gaza Strip – taking Sinai from Egypt and the Golan Heights from Syria. It would take around thirty to forty-five minutes to go from Amman to Jerusalem, a regular commute. These days, it could take all day, and El-Jisir requires Ammo Usama to take me there.

The road to El-Jisir is absolutely mesmerising. Travelling from the hills of Al-Quds (Jerusalem) at over eight hundred metres above sea level, to El-Jisir by Areeha (Jericho) at three hundred metres below sea level, the road is downhill all the way. I remember as a child, Dad would put his car into neutral and allow gravity to guide us almost all the way to Areeha. The land-scape changes fairly quickly from urban to rural small villages embracing the sides of hills, to arid desert-like lunar landscapes with sporadic Bedouin habitations scattered in the small cul-verts and valleys. Late October, the middle of Autumn, the hills are bare, rounded from the winds, scattered with sparse grasses in hues of yellow ochre and small patches of dark viridian where water may have passed.

Along the way, as we travel steeply downhill, the large Israeli settlements such as Giv'at Ze'ev and Ma'ale Adumim loom on our limited horizon. These settlements started off in 1967 as a collec-

tion of caravans, then a few temporary houses which expanded into larger neighbourhoods and are now consid-ered cities in their own right, some with over forty thousand residents each. All the settlements are built on stolen lands. Ma'ale Adumim was built on lands stolen from the towns and villages surrounding Al-Quds: El-Ayzareyyeh (Bethany), Abu Dis, El-Assawiyeh and At-Tur (Mount of Olives). I remember in the '80s when Ma'ale Adumim was rapidly expanding, and the Bedouin tribes that lived in the area were constantly moved on, away from their sources of water. There still are some tribes clinging on to their way of life, but it is getting harder for them to make a living and survive the attacks of hostile settlers who steal their herds of sheep and destroy their water tanks and homesteads.

The road is smooth, newly tarmacked and well maintained, as it is what is considered a settler road, a bypass road that links the various settlements avoiding the Palestinian areas. Since Ammo Usama has a Jerusalem ID card, he drives a car with Israeli number plates, so we are relatively safe, driving on these settler roads.

We chat all the way to El-Jisir. He and I talk about all kinds of things, but mostly about the war in Gaza and its impact on us all. At this point, it has only been three and a half weeks since the beginning of this war. We are still hopeful, and expect it not to last. We reach El-Jisir after Ammo Usama negotiates several checkpoints. It looks empty, with barely any travellers milling about. We wish each other a safe passage and hope that this latest assault on Gaza will end soon, by the beginning of December at the very latest. I pay him what he is due, and he tells me what to expect to pay for the taxi that will collect me from the Jordanian side, which he has arranged on my behalf. A few grateful tears drip from my eyes as I bid him farewell. He assures me I will be okay, and that it is his wajib (duty) to ensure my safety, as I am my father's daughter, bint El Doctor Rustom, the daughter of the Doctor Rustom. The taxi driver who will be waiting for me on the other side, Ammo Usama informs me, is a family friend, who is honest and reliable. His name is Abu Mohammad, first name Saddam.

It's quarter to eleven, and I have arrived at El-Jisir, a word that fills many a heart with dread. Once you say it out loud, you normally encounter expressions of sympathy, offers of telephone numbers of reliable taxi drivers, a flurry of suggestions of how to get through with some dignity. I do not normally choose to go via El-Jisir. Not out of ostentation or superiority, I just try not to, if I can help it. I had not crossed El-Jisir in a very long time. I prefer not to travel via El-Jisir. I really really do not like crossing El-Jisir. It is a humiliating way to travel. You feel insulted, diminished. If I can avoid the extra humiliation, I would rather do that.

I would be humiliated and diminished via El-Lydd Airport anyway. I would be considered subhuman as a Palestinian, according to Israeli racist policies, on par with other non-humans: all nuns and non-white people, such as Asians, black South Africans, Greeks, anyone who has been in touch with Palestinians, in the lands of '48 and the West Bank and Gaza, anyone who looks like an Arab – and all Arabs and Palestinians, naturally. I am usually shielded a little by the British Passport I carry. I just get the sneering dismissive treatment, strip searches, delays and shunning. I make sure I do not wear anything with metal in it, including hair clips. I wear slip-on shoes, elasticated waists, no jewellery; only my silver earrings, and my childhood gold bangle that I cannot remove.

The El-Jisir humiliation can be at a whole different level. I just hope I get the low-level humiliation, considering there are very few travellers today.

I watch my bags being manhandled by the porters who pounce when Ammo Usama stops his car. Ammo Usama suggests, in a whisper, to give them ten shekels discreetly, and they will treat my bags nicely. I am not sure what that means, but I discreetly give them a ten-shekel coin each, and they disappear with my bags, after giving me a sticker for each of them. They smile and point me in the right direction. Ammo Usama waits until I enter, I wave, and a few more tears drip from my eyes.

The entrance looks ominous. The doors are sheets of heavy plastic strips that look like the entrance to a warehouse, or abattoir. They are heavy and slap as you go through them; they hurt a little. Once through, the air conditioning makes me cough. I spot the maze of metal barriers and passageways that guide you to various windows or booths. There is no one in this departure hall except me. I see various windows, but it is not clear what they are for. One appears to be a money exchange, and the other one has a bored-looking woman sitting there. She looks up and signals to me with her long, painted fingernails. I approach. I hand over my passport, she says something in Hebrew, and I ask for English. She looks at me disdainfully, and flicks back my passport. She can't throw it far, as there is bulletproof glass between us, so she has to slide it roughly through the hatch. She points to the money exchange place next to her, with her multi-coloured nails. I wonder if she has too much time on her hands as no one is travelling, and has painted her nails at work.

I go to the next window and show my passport again.

The man behind the glass says, "Two hundred" in a gruff manner.

"Shekels?" I ask.

"Kayn," he says (Yes in Hebrew).

I ask in English, "For what?"

He points wordlessly at a tatty sign saying 'bridge tax'.

I pay the bridge tax, and obtain the receipt.

He points to another booth across the hall, and says in English, "Go."

I cross the hall to the booth he pointed to; it's the passport control booth. I wait behind the yellow-painted line on the ground. There's no one else but me in the hall, and yet the military border person does not call me forward. I wait. I wait for five minutes. I am used to waiting. We Palestinians have perfected the art of waiting patiently. I am called forward, and I hand over my passport. An exit receipt is given back to me with my passport. I walk towards the other booth in the middle of the hall, knowing that must be the way out, judging by the high metal rotating door and wall separating this side from whatever is beyond. I wind my way through more metal barriers. I show the exit pass to another painted-nailed border guard, who barks at me, in Hebrew, and I reply slowly and distinctly: "English please".

She shouts again in Hebrew, and I shrug. She points at something stuck to the bulletproof glass window separating us. I realise she wants the bridge tax receipt, so I show her the receipt I hold in my hand. She looks down on her nails and thumps down on a button to let me through. I wonder if she chipped her nail; I *hope* she chipped her nail with the force she used to press the button, but I don't think she did. Normally, the polite thing to do is mutter a thank you, but I can't be polite. I look impassive, waiting for the buzzing noise that indicates the door mechanism is demagnetised; I walk through the rotating metal barrier, and it clicks closed behind me.

I walk towards what looks like the outside. I look at the hovering random men and wonder, where do I go next? One of the men looks up and asks, "Araby?" (Arabic?) quizzingly.

I say, "Tab'an." (Of course).

He immediately smiles and says, "Come Khalti (my Aunty), here, bus number fifty … where are your bags …"

I point to my bags, which are outside in a cage, neatly stacked. They had treated them kindly after all. One of the men helps me retrieve the bags and puts them on bus number fifty. I give him ten shekels, he says thank you, and I reply with: "Allah ya'teek el Afyeh." (May God give you strength.)

He replies with a smile and the standard "Allah ya'afeeki." (May He give you strength also.) I truly love our Arab courtesy.

I shudder a little – though it is thirty-five degrees (95°F) in the shade with lots of flies and other buzzing insects flying around. What makes me shudder is that I am officially old. I have become a Khalti (my Aunty), not a Yakhti (my Sister). When did that happen? I swipe the buzzing things away. I spot the bus driver and ask him when he is supposed to leave.

He replies, "When there are more of you, are there more in the hall?"

"Not that I have seen."

"Then we wait."

"Do I have enough time to have a smoke?"

"Of course, Yakhti, stay in the shade, it's very hot."

At least I am a Yakhti to someone.

A few minutes later, the bus driver comes up to me and says, "I can help you with the process if you like and you can compensate me."

I ask how much.

"As much as you like."

"I don't know what that means, does that mean ten, fifteen, twenty, one hundred, dinar, dollar, shekel, lira? What do you want and I shall see if I can afford it. What do you want? And what would you do for me?" I have no liras or dollars, and what dinars I have are for the taxi ride to the airport.

"You give what you like", he says.

I reply exasperatedly, "Again, I said, I don't know what that means." I am tearing up at this point. "Ana min hone …" (I am from here.) "Ana 'Udsiyyeh." (I am a Jerusalemite.) "Tistahbilneesh." (I don't like being made a fool.) "La biddi a'ata' Il-Jisir." (I don't choose to come by El-Jisir.) "Wala biddi asafir." (And don't want to leave.) "Bas lazim." (But I have to.) "Fa ma t'azzibni wala t-hoon-ni." (So don't torture and humiliate me.)

My eyes drip a tear, and he says, "I understand, Yakhti, I am from Deir Bzee', you know it?"

I say, "Yes, I know it, it's by Ramallah."

"Yes, so would fifty shekels be okay?" Approximately ten pounds.

I say, "Fine. What will you do for the fifty?"

"I will take your passport, get it to the Jordanian border control, put it on the top of the pile, then get your bags to the taxi that waits for you. It will make it easier for you if I do it."

"Fine." … Fifty shekels for easier passage. Fine.

I smoke a little, look around, no one else is joining me. It has been half an hour in the heat and flies. I climb on the bus. I sit two rows back from the driver. My Israeli e-SIM still has credit, so I check out the Telegram channels I subscribe to, look in horror at what I am leaving behind, and weep silently. I am glad I have a mountain of tissues in my handbag and in my various pockets.

An older man comes on the bus with a small rucksack and sits in front. He had been smoking a cheroot earlier, I thought he was another bus driver. He seems to know the driver, must be a frequent traveller. We wait for another fifteen minutes. I get off the bus again and smoke a little more and swipe at the flies. An American lady comes up, and is unsure where to go. I speak nicely to her, and tell her to climb on, we are waiting for more passengers. She asks what should she do afterwards, and I tell her, "Do what I do, you'll be fine."

She says, "Thank you for speaking in American."

I correct her; I say, "English," and smile.

The bus moves fifty-five minutes after I first sit in it. My brother Dia had been tracking my phone from his phone in Kuwait, and he jumps on the family group chat on WhatsApp to announce: "You are moving, finally."

"Yes, I am moving." It's very strange to be tracked from so far away.

The flies are travelling with us on the bus. They have no restrictions on their travels. Sometimes I wish I was a fly. They seem to focus on the American lady, and I am glad they haven't bothered me, my blood isn't sweet enough I reckon, all the labaneh and za'atar must have an effect. There are only three of us on the bus. The driver declares we cannot wait any longer, and closes the doors. The bus should contain fifty people.

I eke the curtains obscuring the view open, slightly, and try to take a photo of the scene outside. The driver spots me and says in Arabic, "You can't do that, you will have your phone confiscated."

I tell him that I just want to take a photograph of the bridge when we cross it.

He says, "You can't, especially that."

Before we know it, we reach the other side, having crossed the insignificant blink-and-you-will-miss-it bridge. It's not wooden any more, since that bridge was destroyed in 1967 by the Israeli forces. It's just a bit of concrete connecting two tarmacked roads, with a gap below, a trickle of a stream. I did not manage a good photograph of the bridge, but by luck, I got the middle part.

The lunar landscape by the bridge stretches for miles. Tankers line the road on either side obscuring the view. I try to see what kind of tankers they are. They appear to be cement trucks, but the bus rushes past too quickly to tell, slowing down for speed bumps and whizzing on at full speed.

A looming heavy metal gate, partially open, looks ominous. The bus driver pulls up, gets out, addresses the Jordanian border patrol guard – I overhear, "Bass talateh … Amercaan wa Engleezi." (Only three … American and English.) – and climbs back in and drives on. The flies are still buzzing behind me. The poor American woman is getting slightly frantic with her arm movements. The flies must really like her scent.

We reach the Jordanian border post, the other side. The driver asks for our passports, we hand them over and wait. Five minutes later, he comes back and tells us we can get off the bus and escorts us, his three passengers, to the metal detector and luggage X-ray machine. He handles my bags, puts them on the conveyor belt, and I walk through the metal detector. It beeps, I look across to the bored-looking Jordanian soldier, and he just waves me through. I drag my bags off the X-ray machine, and the bus driver points to the booth that says 'Arrivals'. I indicate to the American lady to do the same. The soldier behind the window asks "Leena Rustom? Araby?"

I politely say, "Na'am." (Yes.)

"Ma'aki visa?" (Do you have a visa?)

I say it is on my phone. He makes a gesture of "give it to me".

I open the visa and hand over my phone.

"Where did you travel from?"

"Al-Quds" (Jerusalem).

"You're not from Gaza?"

I answer him: I am not, "Bas laysh tis'al?" (but why do you ask?)

He looks up dolefully and says, "Ghasib anni." (Because I am forced to.) "Leena Rustom, ahlan wa sahlan." (You are welcome.)

I smile and say thank you.

He hands my phone and passport back and adds surprisingly, "Allah yisahhil alaiyki." (May God give you safe passage.)

I reply, "Tislam, shukran, Allah ya'teek el afyeh" (May God give you safety, thank you and give you strength.)

I wish the American lady a safe voyage. She asks me if she can have a lift with me, if I have already arranged my transport, but I decline. I do not feel very generous, which goes against my Palestinian instinct. I am exhausted, worn out by the grief of bidding goodbye to my family and homeland. I do not want to sit with her in a taxi. I do not feel guilty. I point her to where she could arrange for transport to Amman.

I do not have a Jordanian e-SIM to contact Saddam. I hope he will still be waiting. My bags are grasped by a porter, who drags them for me to the other side of the gate, the main road, where Saddam and his car should be waiting. I hand the porter four dinars, and he kisses my hand and says, "Shukran Khalti." (Thank you Aunty.) I am an Aunty again.

That all went surprisingly smoothly and quickly. My anxiety of waiting for hours, with more buzzing flies, not knowing if Saddam would still be waiting, is put to rest. Saddam is full of smiles and oozes kindness. I want to cry. "Ahlan wa sahlan, el hamdillah ala salamtek Khalti" (You are most welcome, thank God for your safe arrival, Aunty.) "Allah yisalmak".

"May I sit in the front with you?" I ask.

"Please, t-faddali."

I climb into his pristinely clean white Hyundai. This is an unusual act. People would usually sit in the back and sit quietly, especially women. But as I am a Khalti, I am going to abuse the situation, use my venerable age, and sit in the front. I want to talk, and Saddam does not disappoint.

The road with Saddam is smooth. "How long would it take to Queen Alia Airport?"

"Around an hour," he says.

Excellent, I have plenty of time.

We talk of many things, of lords and kings – no, not really, we talk just about the situation I had left behind and our views on how things may pan out. His concern is that this crisis will widen and affect Jordan. It inevitably will; with Jordan's population being seventy per cent Palestinian, and Palestinian refugees to be exact, Jordan is bound to be affected.

As he calls me Khalti, I am curious. I wonder how old this man is. I do not feel I can ask directly as that would be too blunt. But I do have a small inkling of when he may have been born. I ask why he is named Saddam. He tells me he was born in 1989 when Saddam Hussein declared his absolute support for the Palestinian Intifada and the PLO, so Saddam was named after him, and he is proud of it.

I say, "And so you should be. It's a good name, a powerful name".

He says his first son was Mohammad and second was Murad (meaning 'wanted'), and if he is blessed with another, he will be called Yasir.

"Good for you," I say. I smile. Resistance can be in small things. Memory can be evoked with little acts, such as naming the next generation.

The Jordanian side of the Rift Valley is lush, green, full of farms. It feels bucolic, it feels agrarian, it feels safe. The road starts to climb steeply towards the Amman hills. Saddam zig-zags his way up, overtaking on the inside and outside lanes of the newly tarmacked highway to Amman. Various highly decorated trucks, laden with produce, are lumbering up the slope, slowly. I can see why he is overtaking. These trucks were not in a particular lane. They take up whichever lane they find themselves on, and stay on it, lumbering under heavy loads of produce, in first or second gear. This creates a slalom-like journey. Saddam is also texting and answering various calls while driving, changing gears with his non-texting hand and steering with his knee. I do not feel unsafe. This feels exactly like the taxi drivers in Palestine. One difference though, is he is wearing a seatbelt. As am I.

We wind our way through the chaotic traffic of Amman, and after an hour and a half, I can see signs for Queen Alia Airport. We arrive at our destination. And I am grateful.

He takes me to the closest point he can get to as a taxi driver. I thank him, and pay him an extra five dinars on top of what I had been told to give him by Ammo Usama, as he had distracted me from the misery of my journey. "Tislami – Shukran." (Thank you – may you be safe.) "Bissalameh, inshallah."(Go with safety – if God is willing.)

I ask if I can call him to ask for a lift when I return a few months from now, and he declares, "Bitsharfeeni, Khalti." (It would be an honour, Aunty.) We exchange numbers. I smile, shake hands, tear up and walk towards the airport terminal. It is half past two. I made it through in record time.

BREAKFAST AT TISSARDMINE

Linda Cracknell

Uncertainty afflicted my rail departure from Perthshire towards Marrakesh. The northern half of Scotland was besieged by early February floods. Water crashed from the hills around my home, roaring down the wooded gorge known as the 'Birks of Aberfeldy' and on to join the river Tay. A moat began to form around the town. I watched the cancellation notices come in on my phone: Pitlochry to London followed by, for no apparent reason, the Eurostar connection to Paris.

It was only the most recent of several public transport upheavals over the winter. I found the fragility of my familiar infrastructure disturbing. Systems were failing; the new climate-crisis weather patterns easily defeating our flimsy show of civilisation. I clung to my phone, searching for other means of travel, teetering on the edge of despair. Should the first day fail, the whole carefully plotted five-day journey was in question. Not only were public transport systems fragile; so was I.

Perhaps, I thought, optimism comes more naturally to the young. But folded within my sixty-four-year-old self were lodged younger selves whose successful solitary missions ought to have bolstered me. Hadn't I traversed Spain's southern mountains in winter with a tent; bussed to the West of Kenya with little by way of a plan?

I was conscious, though, that if I didn't reach Marrakesh in five days' time, I would fail the nine people I was due to meet there.

BREAKFAST AT TISSARDMINE

Our final destination together was a further ten-hour journey, a drive to the Sahara Desert where I was to lead an eight-day workshop in creative writing.

*

Despite all that rickety dread, a lift from a friend took me south to Perth, connecting me to running trains and an earlier Eurostar. I had breakfast the following morning in a café close to Gare de Lyon. The young waitress smiled kindly at me and brought café, jus d'orange and croissant, even filled my flask with hot water. I watched pedestrians flow past, snacking on bread or pastries as they dodged trolleys full of goods unloaded from vans. Now I could stop thinking the worst and entrust myself to the journey. Everything I needed for the next three weeks was on my back; my phone was loaded with timetables and hotel bookings. I could sit back and observe the world.

The airport style check-in process, the two-guns-apiece guards, the news of a knife attack on three people at Gare de Lyon three days earlier were all unsettling. But I was soon comfortably aboard a half-mile long TGV. Paris receded and a low land spread, the sky punctuated by chateaux d'eau declaring 'rural France!' I was plummeting south towards Barcelona, only six hours distant.

The muted winter palette cracked into brightness around Lyon; land rising now, tucking into itself stone buildings of pale terracotta. With the Ardèche to my right, I strained over my fellow passenger on the other side to see the Alps spear up white, foregrounded by dormant vines. A latitudinal boundary seemed crossed into a new sense of season. The hilltop castle of Châteauneuf-du-Pape, maquis and chalk, almond blossom against blue skies. We skirted the Camargue – a place of white horses so beloved on TV in my childhood. A bright flat sea stretched to my left and salty lagoons inland were scattered with pink flamingos. On the far side of the water white towns were stacked up. This journey was also a geography lesson. And all at 292km/h.

Then a tree-clad mountain wall reared ahead and 'whaaoosh', we were under the Pyrenees.

*

I woke abruptly the next morning to the sound of a man sobbing out a nightmare in a room above me, shortly followed by shouting and builders' clatter echoing in the air well. Questions rattled at me: Where am I? Where do I have to get to next?

Gradually the facts settled. I was in Madrid. My next train wasn't until 3pm.

A little later I perched on a stool in a café window savouring the shaking off of everyday responsibility, leaving behind the familiar, becoming a stranger. I'd enjoyed using my sleepy Spanish to order breakfast, culturally distinct to yesterday's: café con leche, zumo de naranja, and tostadas con aguacate y nueces.

As I ate my avocado with nuts and toast and refreshed my adoration for the Spanish way of making coffee, I read an episode from the book I was taking with me into the desert – Antoine de Saint-Exupéry's *Wind, Sand and Stars*. Flying at night, led astray by Saharan radio signals, lost in fog and lofty mountains of cloud on the way to Cisneros (Western Sahara), he and his co-pilot flew in error out over the open sea. They were unsure of their position and had dwindling fuel. Several times they mistook a star for an airfield beacon. They might not even have known if they were flying upside down. Feeling themselves lost amongst stars and planets, they were exposed to nature at its most stark.

Antoine de Saint-Exupéry and I celebrated our salvaged journeys in the same way. He had somehow maintained optimism and foresaw the early-opening café they would find after landing. There they'd laugh off their near disaster with warm croissants and milky coffee. Intense joy was aroused by the scent and taste of milk, coffee and wheat which connected him viscerally to the Earth and its abundance. I like to picture them at this breakfast after their successful landing in Cisneros. A glimpse of the sea through fog had finally turned them back over land, after which they received radio information of more fuel on board than they'd realised, and an instruction to press on.

Thrilled with caffeine and my location, my own anxiety over a minor derailment now seemed ridiculous. And yet, after a fog-drunk passage through space, stars, seas and continents, or having simply overcome public transport disruption, the thrill of being alive is tasted in a good breakfast.

Thinking of ourselves on a planetary scale topples our 'grand' human institutions. Perhaps this is the appeal of the desert and why I was going to Café Tissardmine, a creative retreat centre, for the seventh time since 2012. In the desert, our home on a planet is exposed by wide horizons, vast skies, the human body a small, upright thing on a former seabed; we are proportionate whilst not quite irrelevant. I have felt something similar when at sea and out of sight of land.

Before my afternoon train I visited an exhibition, 'Horizon and Limit', which explored the human relationship with, or invention of, 'landscape'.[3] The contemporary land art collected suggested a rethinking of Romanticism toward something more critical and less elite. A high school group was gathered around a member of the gallery staff, and I stood nearby, listening. She held up the famous image of Caspar David Friedrich's *Wanderer Above the*

3   This exhibition featured a collection of landscape works from the Fundación 'la Caixa' Contemporary Art Collection and was held at Caixa Forum, Madrid.

Sea of Fog (1818), whose subject gazes into sublime mountains, reminding me of the awe that such high terrain can invoke. My Spanish was not up to following it all but I guessed they were being asked to unpack the image and it was hard not to think of the 'lone enraptured male' – a term used by Kathleen Jamie in her critique of male privilege in the outdoors[4] which has contextualised my own solo walks and wanderings.

As I walked Madrid's streets I nodded to former touchstones – yellow post boxes, *El Prado*, the many statues of fabulous beasts. When I was thirty I spent six weeks on teaching practice in a Madrid high school. In the late afternoons I'd wander through the Retiro Park, enjoying the city's rapid transition from bitter frosts into a warm spring. I intended a quick stroll there on my way to Atocha Station but when I arrived, a yellow tape cordoned off the gateway and a sign warned of danger from the trees. I turned away obediently, though I couldn't imagine why or how trees might turn on me.

*

Hill ranges and plains rhymed alongside the trainline towards Algeciras. Great slopes striped with olive trees. I ate an apple, a tangerine, sheep's cheese and the oatcakes I still carried from home, probably a similar picnic to that of my first trip to Southern Spain after my teaching practice finished. Using my phone as today's 'travel agent', I booked my ferry across the Gibraltar Strait for the next day.

As dusk asserted itself further south, a call to prayer hummed from someone's phone and an incremental fusion of cultures was

4   Kathleen Jamie, 'A Lone Enraptured Male', *London Review of Books*, Vol. 30 No. 5, March 2008

reflected in the languages of the carriage. As well as Castilian, I heard Darija (Moroccan Arabic) spoken, and familiar words muttered: "mashi mushkil" (no problem). Andalucia unfolded outside, revealing places I'd explored on former forays south. Còrdoba – the station now flashing past in the rain – still whispering of its former Muslim, Christian, Jewish fraternity, a cathedral built as a cuckoo within a grand mosque. An illuminated screen above me showed the tips of Europe and Africa stretching towards each other like lovers straining toward a kiss.

At 9pm a message on my phone divorced those kissing continents: tomorrow's ferry was now cancelled. I calmed myself as we creaked slowly on into the drenched dark, recalling with shame my response to the last travel uncertainty.

Algeciras station pushed me out amongst pitching palm trees. I crossed a wide, rain-sluiced plaza to reach the port, umbrella gutted by squalls. The ferry company staff couldn't say when the next ship would run; Storm Karlotta was whipping up the Gibraltar Strait and threatened severe westerly gales for several days. It had never occurred to me that weather-related disruption could follow me here.

A little later I dripped onto a hotel desk. The receptionist said: "All this rain and yet we're still on water rationing. And it's early February!"

In Barcelona I'd seen the many 'DROUGHT EMERGENCY' posters, red lettering next to a red bucket, warning people to save water. Winter reservoirs were under sixteen per cent capacity, and Catalonia's eleventh-century church of Sant Romà de Sau, usually beneath twenty-three metres of water, was dry to its foundations. It was likely that water would soon have to be imported, yet hotel guests weren't asked to curtail their showers.

Crossing a swamped patio the next morning, I dodged upturned tables and chairs, pools of blown oranges. A canvas canopy and its metal supports flapped and crashed in each squall. Sirens circled the town. A helicopter. The 'civilised' world tilted off-axis.

Alone at first with the breakfast buffet and with little else to do, I ate pancakes, fruit, yoghurt, toast, eggs. I drank cups and cups of lukewarm coffee as I rebooked my ferry for the following day, but that too was soon cancelled by e-mail.

I phoned Karen, my host at Café Tissardmine. Roughly my own age and British, she's had a long love affair with horizons and wilderness. Since 2010, she's been developing a unique artistic centre, which is her home and also offers visiting artists and writers an experience of the desert alongside the food, creativity and culture of the desert's Amazigh people ('Amazigh' being their own name as opposed to the pejorative, imposed 'Berber').[5] Such is the 'Tissardmine effect' that half our group, all travelling from the UK, had been twice before.

Karen had fully supported my wish to travel by train and was now pragmatic. We agreed to wait and see. If necessary, I could catch up with the group a few days late.

"Or," she said. "I know it defeats the purpose of your train travel, but there's a flight from Malaga to Marrakesh".

I grappled with my resistance to this against my sense of responsibility to the group. By travelling nearly five thousand miles by train rather than flying I'd justified going to Tissardmine once again. I've always valued travel for personal development, getting away from the familiar and finding out about myself as well as other cultures and places. But transport accounts for around one-fifth of global CO2 emissions. Added to this, as a champion of global justice, I knew my 'tourism' was a luxury unavailable to the majority of Moroccans whose personal carbon footprint is far

5   Abdelkader Cheref, 'Don't Call Us Berber, We Are Amazigh', *The National*, January 2024

closer to what every person in the world must aim for in order to stall climate change.

*

From a passport control queue on a gently rocking ferry at lunchtime the next day, I texted Karen: 'I am on an actual ship on sea. It hasn't moved yet but I think it will. So I still hope to join you tonight. Inshallah.'

I'd been at the port since before dawn, awaiting news of sailings, looking out onto a dark rain-slashed road from a café stool with a breakfast of café con leche, orange juice, a pastry. I was now with four other people, each less than half my age, from Germany, France, Denmark and the Netherlands. We had struck up conversation in English at the port, as if recognising commonality in having our luggage on our backs, a way of travelling I prefer – hands free, shoulders back, heart open to the world.

The rain stopped, wind calmed, the sky returned to blue. Algeciras whitened in the sun as we drew away. We spent the crossing comparing stories, lives, locations. We had each made our way to the edge of Southern Europe without flying or driving. Each of us worked or had worked in the sector of care for the Earth – in energy, water systems or conservation. We talked with excitement about our travel plans.

Once I'd bridged continents and our group scattered, I walked the streets of Tangier for the first time. No local data-allowance meant no online maps so instead I asked for directions to the railway station. As usual when in Morocco I approached women who are less likely to insist on accompanying a solo female. Of the several languages spoken here I could get by only in ropey French. The young woman I asked, face framed by her head covering, wore a long, loose gown. She looked plain and serious, but her face grew animated and smiling as she shifted into English and asked me questions about my travels and origins, always curious, she said, about foreigners. She told me she'd learnt English from YouTube videos and was now learning Spanish in the same way. I wasn't in a hurry. Such small verbal interactions make me comfortable in a new place.

At the port I'd seen a long queue of Moroccan women, each struggling to push a heavily-laden trolley of cases and boxes; propelling their whole lives towards Spain. As if straight out of the mountains, they wore boots and their clothing was layered: overcoats on, warm hats over headscarves. Further behind the queue, similar groups huddled on the ground waiting for a later ship. I'd read that with high rates of illiteracy in the Rif Mountains there can be extreme poverty for women, especially if divorced by their husbands. Perhaps these women were heading towards a better salary on Spanish vegetable or soft fruit farms, but these are infamously harsh places where neglect, abuse and overcrowding are common.

I boarded the afternoon TGV train to Casablanca with a renewed sense of my enormous privilege in making this journey. As a freelancer over the last twenty-plus years I've combined a low-income writing life with teaching, involving travel to new landscapes carrying a pen and notebook such as those I now took from my bag.

The ticket inspector, in his crisp dark uniform, his cap banded strikingly with the red and green of the Moroccan flag, approached each table with a soft greeting: 'salaam aleikum'. At Casablanca I changed onto a more traditional train. The toilet was an open hole framing the passing pulse of sleepers; the exterior carriage door was simply left open to allow in a breeze. In the slightly musty second-class compartment, fellow passengers had to shuffle up to wedge me in. I offered around a packet of biscuits, each person refusing with a smile and their right hand held to the heart.

I was delighted at the new certainty of my travel. I would soon be responsible for a workshop; helping people find words to relate to our desert experience. But not yet. Not even tomorrow. After a night in Marrakesh, we would set off by road at 8.30am.

In the early evening, dusty plains, sheep, silos, minarets passed. An orange line across a green slope, scored by human feet. Olive trees. A donkey cart next to a concrete motorway intersection. On station platforms, men kissed cheeks in greeting, walked away hand in hand. In the seat next to me a young woman, sleek in a leather jacket, black leggings slashed at each side with a transparent panel, watched a film on her phone demonstrating the hennaing of patterns onto hands. When I stood up approaching Marrakesh, she helped me lift my rucksack from the rack.

Waiting to disembark in the train's lobby, I was pushed up against another young woman and her head-scarfed mother who had a curly-haired grandson of about one year strapped in a large cloth to her back. I'd seen several three-generation families like this on the train. The boy leant back and fixed me with an upside-down stare – huge eyes circled with dark lashes. We made a game of it – me hiding my face with my hands and then revealing it. The two women laughed along. After disembarking myself, I turned to help the older woman with her bulky luggage, lifting the bag down narrow, steep steps onto the platform. All smiles, she blew me a kiss and I said: 'mashi mushkil'.

Not having children myself, I haven't participated in the intergenerational rhyme so evident here. This has always made me feel somehow 'ageless'. Such familial markers of life events and roles are absent from my daily living. But it was as if on this journey I was realising my actual age; a good one for travel in Morocco, where elders are respected and there is less likelihood of sexual harassment for older women.

Was I also becoming a bit vague and forgetful? I'd left my phone in the scanner at St Pancras Station, causing an official to run after me; I woke every morning wondering: What city? What room? What layout? Where's the loo? When I asked a question of a stranger – for confirmation or directions – I'd been bobbing my head and raising a forefinger at the answer as if to say 'got you' or 'I thought so'. This gesture of my mother's as she got older had irrationally irritated me with its old-lady-ish-ness, yet here I was adopting it myself.

*

A serrated line ran across the sky to the east of Marrakesh: the High Atlas Mountains, raised by snow into a mythic-seeming barrier. Our newly-met group were driven in a minibus towards it as early morning mist jewelled any leafy groundcover. We wound up through dusty grey and red earth and the flat-topped buildings of the villages. The sun rose fat from the mountains and its low light began to carve spurs of rising land into animal limbs. Two men in long wool djellabas drank coffee within the arched porch of a squat pink house in the first, frost-thawing, sunlight. We passed a sudden shock of oranges piled up on a village stall, and a donkey, panniers weighed down with sacks of flour.

After the high, zigzagging passes, we followed a broad river-bed, its dry rivulets and corridors of golden rushes telling the story of earlier watercourses. Decaying kasbahs were encircled by palm trees, their blocky walls of pink mud thrilling against a backdrop of red escarpment, snow-topped mountain, blue sky. Time and the long road to Morocco's east was paid out like lengths of rope, measured by police checkpoints, mosque minarets, phone masts.

Our small bus at first buzzed with chat. Later, the journey slipped each of us into silent, private periods on the long road.

For the next ten days we would be together, the sandwich filling between my solitary journeys overland between here and Scotland. Already the logistics of my return train journey were falling away, lost beyond a hazy horizon.

Onwards after Ouarzazate – the High Atlas now parallel to our left – through the Draa valley, rose fields in winter. Past towns like Tinghir, an oasis once under the sea and now wedged between two mountain ranges. The road unspooling and unspooling. My thoughts freed by motion and little to do.

In the late afternoon the sun lowered and sand blew up, turning the light milky. A woman facing backwards on a tuk-tuk held her black headscarf over her nose and mouth, leaving just a slot through which she squinted into the sinking sun.

Distances between settlements widened. Long flat miles were interrupted only by reptilian crags and signs for fossil tours; the territory of extinct marine arthropods from 521 million years ago. The sea seemed only just out of sight. In Erfoud the golden hour was enjoyed by women strolling or sitting cross-legged in small groups with their children on open ground. We cast off from here, the port town, into the Sahara. Our driver, sensing sundown and his desert home, picked up speed.

A journey was drawing to a close six days after I'd left home.

*

For the next eight days I would circle a small radius. Although Tissardmine was known and familiar to me, I 're-cover' it for myself each time I come: the ebb and flow of light and temperature, the pleasing rhythm of meals, workshops, occasional group excursions, conviviality. We are pared back to essentials: food, drink, soul, body. It's impossible not to be aware of our location on a planet – the stars insist it, the roll of the horizon, the turn of day and night.

I set out before sunrise the next morning for my usual solitary walk, leaving Tissardmine's walled enclosure all quiet, to cross a rubbled valley which holds the salt-crusted memory of the river Saf-Saf. I walked east, finding the familiar ridge to follow, a raised band of tipped-up strata; snaking tiers of rising and falling rock interspersed with shimmery slopes of blown sand. My nose ran in the morning cold as I crouched down to study the winding lace-trails laid by beetles and lizards across pristine sand, the chiselled texture of rocks amongst yellowy-gold bushes forming spiky balls. I picked up a stone that had clearly been 'cooked' at some point – its spongy elastic appearance like well-risen bread baked into something like glass.

I enjoy here a sense of being distant from human civilisation and permitted by slight elevation a glimpse into the milky-skied, vast, 'beyond'. A distant wall of crags ahead represent to me the equivocal 'border' with Algeria. The scale, before you have learned this place at all, can be unnerving. An indomitable mountain abruptly shrinks to a small mound with the appearance upon it of a giant figure or vehicle. Height and distance are distorted by lack of familiar comparatives. I'd walked less than a mile and could still see 'home'.

In the night I'd felt the silence like a lid, solid and dense. Then somewhere towards morning came a low growl as if echoing from deep under the earth itself. The village call to prayer. Out here on the ridge a barely-detectable static buzzed as I waited.

Illumination began above the 'Algeria' ridge: the sun pale through sand-haze but rising fast, soon polishing the rock to blue. A spiny, ribbed fossil was defined between my feet, pointing like a finger directly towards the sun – a glorious ship launching. A tide had turned, prompting the piping of an unseen bird behind my shoulder – perhaps a white-crowned wheatear. Distant chicken crow, donkey bray, the whine of a motorbike engine washed in from somewhere 'beyond'.

I turned back across the stone-bristled plain. White Saharan lilies graced the curving runnels made by vehicle tyres or where water had run; opportunists. My hat was off and I was hungry. Tissardmine and breakfast and chat and laughter were tangible around the mosaic-topped patio table ahead. There would be coffee, omelette with rich tomato sauce under the egg, rounds of warm bread, cheese, salty black olives, fig jam, shared as the slant of the sun changed and our fingertips warmed.

The length of shadows would then become the day's clock.

WHAT IT IS TO STAY

Amanda Thomson

I'm trying to write into the idea of travel, and thinking of movement beyond the UK, but I find myself thinking more about what it is to stay. It's complicated, all these goings and returns seen in retrospect, and through a lens that encompasses not just physical distances travelled, but people met and the passing of time.

I wonder why we go. For simple curiosity? The experience? A change from our normal routine? The photos we can show on our return? The stories that we gather to tell? If we write them for consumption by others, does that count for more? For cultural connections and conversations, to reconnect with distant friends and family, or for the heat in our bones? Do we go because it's what we, as a species, have always done? Who's to say what counts and what does not. As we're encouraged to reduce our carbon footprint, to consider the ethics of travel and tourism, it's easy to forget that so many families and peoples have been dispersed across the world through no fault of their own; the world is full of different diasporas. Without the freedom of travel, the lack of physical connection to more distant family or your ancestral home might splinter your very identity. And sometimes visiting places that are elsewhere can give you what you might need, even crave, to feel at home. Some experiences and encounters will make you understand yourself better, and help you become who you need to be.

There's a family trajectory to Madrid and Spain that predates my own time there, predates even my birth. It starts in the late 1950s, when my mum was there, and punctuates my childhood: her photograph albums; a record, *Guitars Galore*; an art book about the Museo Del Prado that I'm sure has Velazquez's *Las Meninas* on the cover (though when we looked recently we couldn't find it); a Julian Bream record, his classical guitar playing the music of Rodrigo. When I think back, the images of Madrid I held were first in black and white: wide streets and beautiful parks, windows with slatted shutters, street cafés, bustling plazas and strong coffees and swirls of cigarette smoke. Impossibly slim women in large print dresses and bouffant hair-dos, dapper men in double breasted suits or open neck shirts and slicked back hair. The moments when my mum reminisced about her time in Spain must have been very sporadic, the albums full of photographs brought out perhaps once a year, not even that, and probably at my request. The images stuck with me. I must have held them close as a possibility of something, somewhere else, somewhere other, even at a time when, in my own childhood, I never went north of Perth – never mind outside Scotland.

As we look through the photo album again in 2024, Mum shakes her head, laughs and talks about her and Doris, the pal she travelled with, as 'innocents abroad'. She describes a group she calls the Plaza Santa Ana gang, folk from all over, gravitating to Spain, and a very different Spain then to now too. She remembers meeting two guys from the States and how they wore Levis, the first time she'd seen anyone in jeans. There were writers, teachers, young people straight and gay, all interested in travelling to someplace new, to be somewhere which was not home. Mum shows me a receipt of the first trip she and Doris made, travelling to Paris, then from Paris to Madrid and on to an Academy in Cádiz to learn Spanish, staying with a family when they did so. Two air returns from Glasgow to Paris, two couchettes from Paris to Irun, flights from Madrid to Seville, hotels … the total cost of that trip: ninety-nine pounds, ten shillings and sixpence. How they must have planned, dreamt, saved.

She talks about going to Mallorca and to Palma Nova across the bay with a father and son on their wee boat, and about how it was just a beautiful beach with a couple of parasols stuck in the sand; places that are now massive tourist resorts were not much more than fishing villages. She recalls the time her heart was in her mouth when the police took her and a Spanish friend to the police station for an innocent display of affection on the street – a laugh as he put his arm around her shoulder as they walked – and how the police were paid off with some pesetas. This was Franco's Spain, a military dictatorship, and they had to be careful. *We were pioneers*, she tells me, *there weren't any cheap holiday type packages, we just decided to do it, in our youthful exuberance.* I ask who was more adventurous, her or Doris, and she replied that she couldn't remember who egged the other on, because in later life neither one of them would be so brave, and it's something I can totally relate to now I'm older. *Youthful exuberance.*

Madrid holds jumps in time for us. My mum, there in the late '50s, my own time there teaching English in the late '80s, and then a few days back in 2023, just passing through. I look at my mum's photos again and see how remarkable they are – my mum standing in the Plaza de España, with more than a sixty-year time gap between that photo and when I was there last. Another photo is of a street that looks like it's one of the ones leading to the Plaza Mayor, and it's a photograph I could have taken last year. There's a photograph of a donkey and cart on the kerbside of a wide street, and when I look closely at the buildings behind it I see that mum's taken it at Puerta del Sol, the very centre of Madrid, from where all the streets of the city emanate – now an epicentre of noise and taxis and cars and people. I've stood in a crowd there at Hogmanay, each of us eating a grape for good luck at each of the twelve bell tolls at midnight, seeing in the new year.

My own memories of my time in Madrid are in technicolour, hazy with heat and cigarette smoke and probably too much to drink, as well as time and distance. When I look at my own photographs we all look so young, my hair's wild and becoming dreadlocks, shaved sides, my Soul II Soul phase. I can't quite remember the impetus behind my own travels there, apart from an idea of Madrid that I'd held close since childhood, and ending university with no idea what to do, no jobs on the horizon. And, of course, the need to escape Britain under Thatcher, Section 28, the Poll Tax. And perhaps, with a friend, our own youthful exuberance to seek out something and somewhere else.

Sometimes travelling can feel like being in a bookshop, when you think you know what it is you're looking for, but you come away with something completely unexpected and different. Or you go in to kill time, not quite knowing if you are looking for anything at all in particular, yet leave with something quite unexpected and amazing, and perhaps life changing.

To live in a city like Madrid, after a small-town childhood home and even a city like Edinburgh, felt like a complete expansion of my world. The heat, the outsideness of everything made the whole place feel convivial. I recall neighbourhood festivals and generations dancing sevillanas together. Everything closed in the afternoon for siestas and we started teaching again at 4pm, finishing about eight or nine. We ate incredible tapas with our cañas – calamares, pulpo, gambas al ajillo, and paella of course, dishes that my now vegetarian self won't eat but at the time I absolutely loved. We spent time in neighbourhood bars and cafés, traditional and new. Chueca was the gay district but closer to our barrio was No se lo digas a nadie (don't tell anyone about it), a women-run bar/ club with, I seem to recall, a feminist book shop upstairs. Closer still were *Café Barbieri*, an old, traditional bar where an elderly lady in the back sold cigarettes, and *Soidermersol*, a restaurante económico, perfect after a long day's teaching. I loved how the city opened up at night, as busy at midnight as at rush hour. And, like my mother before me, I met people from all over Spain and all over the world. One hot summer's evening in the Retiro, Madrid's massive park, I listened to an open-air orchestral concert; I still have the programme, Junio 1989: Orqueste de Cámara 'Reina Sofia' playing 'Homenaje a Joaquín Rodrigo'. It was the music I'd listened to in childhood – *Fantasia para un gentilhombre, Concierto de Arajuez* – and I remember even now a feeling of coming in some kind of full circle, and wondering what would come next.

Darryl, Gerry and Ricky were migrants from the US, three African American gay men who had landed up in Madrid. I'm not sure why there, but some clues were in the stories they told of the gay community in New York which they were part of in the 1980s, the number of friends they knew who had died or were dying of HIV and AIDs. I imagine they wanted to find some respite from the grief and loss they'd already encountered as young men. I met them perhaps a year into being in Madrid, when it was clear that me and the pal that I'd travelled with were on different trajectories, and I was looking for a new place to stay. Alison was teaching in one of the schools I worked at and was looking for a roommate, so I ended up sharing with her and Darryl in the Lavapiés barrio of the city, close to El Rastro, the huge Sunday flea market that wound its way down Lavapiés. Our apartment was unbelievably hot and airless in the summer months. It had a bright red living room, crazy ornaments and an open interior shaft between each of the apartments that held the laundry lines. The sounds of someone practicing the classical piano drifted up and wafted in, the aromas of fried fish and chicken also. Cockroaches scuttled underneath the lift when you entered the building and the light came on.

When I met Darryl, and then Ricky and Gerry, suddenly I was with people who shared so many cultural touchstones with me, though the countries we came from were different. Slightly older than me, they took me under their wing. I felt an enormous affinity with how they talked about racism and homophobia, and the experiences of their lives. Gerry and Ricky were a couple, artists who'd set up a makeshift studio in their apartment. In between teaching they would paint, and they encouraged me to do the same. There was something about being removed from our home countries, and being different together, perhaps, that bonded us too. I can't remember all of what we talked about, except that we went out a lot, cooked and ate and drank and danced and laughed a lot. Darryl, Ricky and Gerry were so much more extrovert than me, I loved their outrageousness and their unmediated outrage at the world, its racism and heteronormativity. And, in a time before the word was coined, they taught me about intersectionality and how to be in the world; how to be me in the world, even, learnings that I took with me when I went home to Scotland.

I visited Darryl a year or two after he moved back to Washington DC. It was my first time going to the States and encountering US border control: where was I going, who was I visiting, what did I do, when was I leaving? Was Darryl my boyfriend? What did he do? I saw another Black woman, French-speaking I think, who'd sat in a seat along from me in the same row of the plane, escorted off to a side room. I was relieved to get through. Once in the city, discovering it for myself as Darryl went to work, I remember feeling so at home, almost immediately, and more so than I'd ever felt on any visits to London or any other places with more people of colour than I usually encountered in Scotland. There was the heat, so familiar from living in Madrid, but, especially after returning to Scotland, there was the ease I felt walking the streets of Adams Morgan and Dupont Circle, going to the Smithsonian Museums, visiting the National Gallery of Women in the Arts and being surrounded by people who *looked like me*. Bars and cafés and restaurants where I was not the exception. Bookshops where Angela Davis, Audre Lord, Toni Morrison, Alice Walker and Ntozake Shange were front and centre, not afterthoughts or in niche displays. I have a potent memory of walking back to Darryl's apartment alone late one evening after being out at a bar, and for the first time feeling that my colour protected me and made me feel safer. It was not something that I would be called out or abused for.

We went to bars where at least half of the clientele were African Americans, to *Meskareen* in Adams Morgan, the restaurant where my mind was first blown by the injera and wats that make up the foods of Ethiopia. I've a photo somewhere of Darryl and I sitting on the porch of Frederick Douglass's house. I can still taste the smoky aubergine slices and baba ganoush in pita bread from a late-night take-out close to a bar we used to go to. One night, a gang of us went to Bachelor's Mill, a club on the south-east side of the city, predominantly for and full of African American gay men, that had inside and outside dance floors and somewhere off the dance floors a bar/ café that sold fried chicken and fries. The club played the most incredible, joyous gospel house/ dance music, and I remember still the incredible feeling of release, happiness, freedom. It occurs to me that sometimes we travel to find a place where we can feel more at home, or at home in a different way. It can be a relief, sometimes, to leave where we live behind, at least for a little while. Sometimes you don't realise how tightly you hold yourself, even in familiar places, until you go someplace where you can be a little looser, and find another part of yourself.

My partner is from the US, and for the years when we went to visit her family, at a time before the Civil Partnerships or gay marriages were possible, our journeys back and forth held a feeling of trepidation. Once there, Chicago had that big North American city multicultural feel that you can't beat. Getting there, however, with her US passport and my UK passport, meant that at each border we would have sometimes an hour and a half of separation as we went through immigration, each of us fast tracked at one end or the other, no way of communicating, just hoping that we would get through, even though our passports, visas and travel documents were legitimate. The wait in line always held the stressful possibility that completely unknown people could upend our lives, even if the sheer luck of where we were born, our jobs and our social status made that unlikely.

In the years when my partner's parents were still alive, we'd bookend our visits to Chicago with different US road trips, to the South-West in particular, creating a new tradition of always stopping at every Iron Skillet diner we saw. More than a decade's worth of travel that took in Flagstaff, Arizona; Santa Fe; Taos; Albuquerque in New Mexico; Bryce Canyon; Canyonlands and Arches; a strange road trip from Chicago through Utah to the Bonneville Salt Flats; and on to Wendover, Nevada. Long car journeys on interstates, where it felt like we were chasing the same cloud for hours, were punctuated by vireos and tanagers and belted kingfishers, red-tailed hawks, cactus wrens, turkey vultures, bald-headed eagles, egrets, hummingbirds, whip-poor-wills: everyday birds there, but completely new to us. I remember standing on the rim of Canyon de Chelly, part of the Navajo Nation, after a hot, parched hike down to the cliff dwellings at its base, watching an incredible thunderstorm hitting the far rim, and countless thick waterfalls almost instantaneously appearing. We went to the South Rim of the Grand Canyon in September and watched the raptor migrations: the canyon itself impossibly huge, the raptors impossibly high, and we read Terry Tempest Williams and Leslie Marmon Silko, who made us so aware of the circumstances that made all of these places as they were and us able to travel to them in the way that we could.

I remember the wet heat of the Deep South and the sheer scale of the Mississippi, delicious gumbos and beignets and a brilliant conversation about Michelle Ndegeocello in a record shop in New Orleans and buying her newly released 'Cookie: The Anthropological Mixtape' on CD that we played on repeat. How the street music and general vibe of the French Quarter of New Orleans was completely at odds with the abiding memory of travelling up-river to Natchez, Mississippi, and the feeling of a whole restaurant full of white folks falling silent and looking at us when we walked in; being suddenly very aware of seeing very few, if any, interracial couples, never mind a gay couple; in the entire road trip through Louisiana and Mississippi, never quite being sure that we were safe.

We laugh about the idea of having a gaydar, an intuition that helps you sense other people who are gay, but there's a sixth sense you develop that acts as a warning signal too, a sense of when you need to be more careful. One year we took a thousand-mile road trip from Manhattan, a small town in Kansas where we were visiting family, to the North Rim of the Grand Canyon via the Oklahoma panhandle and New Mexico. The whole trip we'd make decisions on whether my white partner would be the one who'd go into the gas stations to pay for fuel. Back then, we held questions about whether it was okay to book double as opposed to twin beds – everywhere, including in Scotland and the UK. We found the Purple Roofs website which listed gay-owned accommodation and, when we could afford it, spent a bit more just to know we'd be safer. It felt like we were buying ourselves out of prejudice, perhaps, and we felt lucky when we were able to do so. I've a male friend who regaled me with a story of him and his wife being taken to some out of the way place by locals in a far-flung country to experience 'authentic' music and food, becoming completely lost and taken advantage of in the process. It made for a fabulous story, but I have to wonder at how much (white) straight, or straight-passing couples can do – can get away with doing – that I think for me and my partner, or other women, would be seen as foolhardy, if not stupid. And I know we limit ourselves, sometimes, before we should.

I recall another trip, an incredible experience travelling through Morocco with another woman of colour, my partner at the time. I remember being cautious, again, of our body language; the sweetness of mint tea and the aromatic scents of tagines; the busyness and the hot, sweet, spicy air of the souks. I recall the sounds of the calls to prayer at the end of the day and how they drifted and mingled in the air and the different quality of the light. When we arrived back at the Spanish Border, while the white travellers were waved though and back into Spain with a flash of their passport, the border guards made us wait for an almost interminable time before allowing us back into Europe.

So I'm really aware that, as I write this, I'm abutting negative experiences with so many of the positive things that come with travel, and that's perhaps indicative of the bittersweetness that comes with it too, and how it reflects the complexities of the world and who and how we are in it.

I feel lucky to have travelled most at a time when we perhaps didn't think enough about what it is to travel: when the climate emergency wasn't so front and foremost our minds. Most of my going now is in and around Scotland, and I don't have an urge to travel much further afield, though I do still, occasionally. But I find myself conflicted about how and where my curiosity, my needs, my varying status (as a person of colour, a lesbian, a 'professional', a British citizen and everything that means) might allow me to go, and where in the world it feels safe to travel to, and whether I should go. The United States, a place I've largely loved visiting, which has meant so much to me and who I am over the years, a place that that holds family and friends still, is in the throes of a backlash against Black Lives Matter. It is a place where Black and queer histories are being rewritten and erased and books are being banned and the swing to the right and against women's rights is terrifying. There are over sixty places still in the world where homosexuality is against the law. I've no doubt that my status as a tourist sometimes confers me more privilege and comfort than those who live in the places where we might travel to. And I am conflicted about how some of us are able to choose to travel so easily when so many others are being so forcefully displaced or denied movement. There's an inherent 'us' and 'them' to travelling, and there can be an extractiveness and a transactionality of encounter that can feel complicated, too.

I'm lucky to live in Scotland, with family and friends close by, in a place that I love, with nature and wildlife that fascinate me and so much so close to me in coasts, mountains and cities. I live in the Highlands, where people travel to from all over the world, close enough to the North Coast 500 tourist route, to Highland 'beauty spots' too. I know what it is to experience those who come, for good and for ill. I see, from the other side, what people get out of visiting. I also see the congestion, the faux Scottishness that panders to an ideal of what this country is but doesn't usually include its complexities. I think about the great conversations I have with visitors from other places, in pubs and trains and cafés, at the tops of mountains, and what I get from the authors, artists and musicians that bring their words and work and music to us. We can get so much of the world from here too, but sometimes we need to take ourselves to new places. I wonder, without travel, who I might have become.

I think of how aging is a form of travel itself, less precise, more complicated and as much about forgetting as having moments of recollection. Looking back at photos taken in Spain over six decades ago, my mum can still remember some of the names of the people she met, where people came from, personality traits, moments of adventure, funny stories. How hard her heart pounded when she was taken to that police station. I think that her travels have helped make her who she is, sustain her in many ways and, at eighty-eight, still inform her curiosity and her outlook on life. She can still speak Spanish way better than I ever could.

Wandering through Madrid in 2023, the city felt so familiar and I found Soidemersol and Café Barbieri again, but though I found the street I couldn't quite remember the entrance to my old apartment building, and I couldn't quite put the geometry of the city together; couldn't always find the places that I held as snapshots in my head. But while many of the specificities were lost, I'd a real feeling of warmth towards the city, and I realised that I'd carried what it had given me in all the years since I stayed there. My mum hasn't been back to Madrid or Spain since her time there in her early twenties, over six decades ago, but there's parts of Madrid and Spain that we both still hold close, moments that we can each remember with absolute clarity. I love how, when she talks about streets and plazas, I can conjure her there through having been there myself, and her memories intermingle with my own. Our travels remain with us, sustain us and make us who we are, bond us across time and space. Sometimes, it is the going away that helps define what it is to stay.

STAY AT HOME

Sarah Thomas

I sink my hands into the needles of spruce, comb through their multitudes with my fingers.

They glide over my fingernails like grains of wild rice, but lighter: the weight of solid air, copper-coloured, a tobacco scent unleashed by my touch. My palms make a furrowed circle around me, arms outstretched across earth's thin but vital skin. The ground is a dry and soft forest bed; springy, unassuming.

And yet it holds my everything: sit bones sink and settle, ankles cross and knees relinquish. Back finds a mossy prop against a trunk. Sunlight finds my face and makes rainbows of my lashes. It lulls my eyelids downwards, un-focusing my gaze.

I turn inwards and outwards all at once, the distinction evaporated. Around me spruce trunks stand tall, their uprights a rhythm in an unfolding understory. Some fallen ones lean on those still living. Or the living support the falling ones to fall gently; to become something else. From this spot down on the forest floor, it appears as if they have gathered round to listen. Behind me a tree creaks, deep as a frog.

This needle bed holds my everything: my sitting bones, my over-active head, my armfuls of uncertainty and blood-rushes of fear begin to loam into darkness, disintegrate a finger-fathom deep. A breeze comes through from the estuary – the greening crowns rock, and sigh, and whisper; shafts of light pierce the canopy in searching beams – and it meanders around the trunks to where I'm sat. It scatters a confetti of spruce shoot husks into the air, and the light finds them there. These tiny translucent copper cups dance, spiral, fall, chase one another onto the sea of needles, find stillness clustered in a hollow. Dappled by sun, the surface layer is warm and dry, a cloak for the moist transformations beneath – the changing states which nurture life on this rocky peninsula. I take a pinch-full of needles, rub them between thumb and forefinger, drop them from a height. They rock and float, boat-like, down a river of air that mingles with my breath.

Heron signals her return in a single *kaaar*. Her chicks respond: click their urgent need *click-click-click*, the sound of quartz pebbles knocked together, and within a long second – the broad sweep of her primordial shadow plays across the needles. I lift my gaze to the blue sky opening to watch her easeful, feathered craft of a body circling the canopy. Her legs trail behind, light as a record player's tonearm, her talons a stylus tracing the wind's music. In a fanning of wings, she lands in the high-perched nest. Her legs pick their way into this screeching, tumbling cacophony of survival held together by a circle of twigs. Her neck flexes a question mark; raises the fish which she had swallowed head-first to swim down the river of her oesophagus. Now she sends them back, upstream; gurgles them into the young ones' expectant and needy bodies. And then she leaves again, back to the brackish water's edge. Back to stand still, watching – and waiting.

*

Beyond this place, through these trees, up the avenue of broom and past the beech whose downy leaves percuss the drizzle like static: that man. Beyond this place, across the floodplain fields of newborn lambs and the crab apple tree standing like a squat, pink-blossomed sentinel: that man. That neighbour from across the road who stands in front of his bungalow or paces up and down the street talking to himself, beer can in hand. Beyond this place, along the lane past the hedgerow – fiddlehead fern, jack by the hedge (mustard, peppery on my tongue), dock, cleavers – the village, complicit: *ach he's got schizophrenia.* Their unwillingness to intervene is dangerous, both to him and to me. The orange brick gatepost: is he there? No. Good. Up the pace, along the pavement past the shop. Home. Shut the door. Breathe.

Beyond this place there are forces circling, visible and invisible. *Stay at home,* they say. But the response to this virus – this heightened, weird, unwieldy time – warps and amplifies. Whatever state you are in, it makes more of it. *Stay at home.* What if those walls, meant to keep us safe, ricochet your fear that he will again come over from across the street when you try to go for a walk, as if he was waiting for you to appear, stepping across the two-metre boundary that has become your sanctioned realm, saying words that make no sense and yet are terrifying to you? What about the threat that, in order to stay distant, you have to step back each time he comes forward, unable to stand your ground? The terror of what that gesture actually means; what's going on in his mind as he slices his hand across his throat? The horror at how the neighbours downplay it and let me know that I *won't want to be the one making the phone call, being an incomer n'all.* What if those walls don't offer a sense of refuge and you need to get beyond them, to a kind of home that holds you safe?

Outside of this haven of spruce and heron and changing sea, I come apart: my body is a jostling crowd of cells which collide and fizz, my blood sour, as if I am inhaling particulates of confusion. These pieces of me thrum with an historic rupture: the first time in my lifetime that so many have felt truly vulnerable, all at once.

*

I have lived with the anxiety of a kind of collapse for many years, but that was worry for the unravelling of the very matrix in which we are held: *the living world, nature, the environment, the biosphere, the ecosystem* ... all these terms which keep us at a safe distance from the pain that surfaces when you call this planet what it is: Home. The ecological crisis has been evident for decades but, until surprisingly recently, many could not or did not want to see it. Do we even have the tools to deal with the grief that would come with that seeing, and with tracing that muddy river upstream to our own broken relationship with ourselves?

I have attended courses, conference and festivals exploring how we might practice resilience to collapse, how we might respond creatively. It has formed the basis of long conversations with friends and colleagues. But all the ideas that emerged from those conversations assumed a possibility of being with others. I did not imagine a time when a virus would make coming together the one thing we could not do. Of all the things I took for granted that have fallen away, this has caught me unawares. Being together: deemed a risk to life as a virus that did not evolve with us looks for new hosts.

Stay at home. All of a sudden, the rush and noise of our lives are paused. For once, we can hear voices other than our own and our engines'. The roads are mostly empty of cars. The sky is free of air traffic – blue without contrails, clear without jet sound. In its place, most noticeable is the exalted bubbling of birds in Spring. Out of sight, the low frequency hum of global shipping has been curtailed. Marine acousticians are seizing this rare opportunity to record how complex are the sentences of uninterrupted whales. Time has changed shape and behaviour too. I do not experience it marching on, blinkered, heedless of its destruction. Instead, it pools and curdles, wrapping around itself like the colours in an oil patch.

This pause holds me in a strange suspension. It finds me in the middle of an artist residency but with no income. It finds me not knowing how to process this experience; not knowing what kind of world I am responding to. At low tide on this south-west Scottish coast of tidal inlets, the sea retreats far into the Solway Firth, leaving an expanse of silt and sand, thick with bivalves and worms. If you know the areas where the sand is firm, it is possible to walk from one peninsula to the next, across the seabed, suspended in a moment that will vanish soon enough. Every six hours, sand becomes sea becomes sand again. It is a landscape, seascape, which is not this and not that. Both this, and that. Perhaps it is the perfect place to be in this long moment.

*

Now my mandated world is five miles wide, I have decided to give up my car, to take it off the road completely. I want to know what it feels like to move through the world on foot, at the pace at which we evolved. I want to know what I hear, feel, notice, travelling at that pace. And I want to know if it is true that our hearts beat to the rhythm of our movement.

This is how I found the herons, moving like this, drifting through the woods down the yellow avenue of broom. I heard them as I stopped to inhale the blossoms' scent, and the lazy saunter of two bees' flight droned a minor third about my head.

Click-click-click.

This is why, noticing my heartbeat and my movements slowing, I stayed in the woods longer each day. At first, I came for my daily walk, riddled with anxiety. Later, I brought coffee and my journal to write; noticed the anxiety fading for a while. Soon after, I extended my possibilities by bringing a rucksack with lunch and my work – pens, notebook, laptop, camera. Passing my days here in the woods created a calm, flat place between the spikes of crippling panic, and the hypervigilance that started outside my front door and continued most of the way to the heronry, until I could hide myself inside the tumble of trees. The herons' screeching soothed me; embodied the urgent clash of my feelings so that I didn't have to; offered me consonance and catharsis that I found nowhere else.

Corra-ghritheach (Gaelic).

Corra – heron or crane, derived from the old root kar, to scream.

Ghritheach – learned or wise.[6]

This is how I found them, and then learned to be with them, as they learned to be with me.

*

The recent rain hushes my footsteps as I enter the wood – no crack of sticks. The moss is soft and presses back. I stand at a distance from the tree as a parent comes to feed the chicks; let them see me. Their screeching begins immediately. Though it is a deeply unpleasant sound, I am invested now in the life force it speaks of. My heart soars to hear it. The feeding happens in a flap of wings and flex of neck, then the parent is off again.

Sure enough, three young ones are standing up in the nest, preening, perching. Around them, trunks and branches squeak with swaying, the canopy a dance of space and form. One chick flutters out and lands on a nearby bough. It allows itself to be moved by the branch, while itself remaining completely still. Deciphering more now in the cacophony that greets an inbound parent, I realise that there is another nest higher up. I see a jumble

6   Robin Hull, *Scottish Birds: Culture and Tradition,* Mercat Press, 2001

of twigs that does not look like a viable structure for the weathers it may have to face. And from sound, though I cannot see it, I become aware of a third nest, level in the canopy with the first. A community of herons: perched between earth and sky where a river meets the sea.

I enter quietly but make myself known. Greet them. Read the ground for recent heron events. I sit quietly, my back against a trunk, watching, and waiting. Early on, there was a temptation to record, photograph, film this exquisite privilege. But it rarely worked. The herons are perceived only in glimpses. If I entered that frame of mind to capture, if I pulled out a device, they would quieten, disappear, retract the curve of their necks back into the weave of sticks. Over time I have learned that the best way to take this life in is to be with it, to stay with it.

*

A white twig lies, like a fine bone, caked in guano – matte, like porcelain. And another, and another; a spring clean from the nest above. *How much shit is too much?* I imagine her thinking. New twigs are in ample supply, to be woven into this becoming. These white twigs are light and smooth, the way that driftwood feels different to forest wood – like ghosts and fossils all at once. States, matters are finding each other and making something new that we have not yet trapped in the wrong name. What rhythm do these two twigs want to make when I tap them together?

There is half a broken eggshell too, a pale turquoise blue, larger than a hen's egg. The inside is a delicate white, slicked yellow with yolk. A light breeze rolls it to the right, and rolls it back again. The herons are making room in the nest; making it comfortable to grow.

There is a feather, a dark one – ragged, with a single spot of guano. *Do you know the perfume of a heron feather?* Like musk.

Like the inside of old books. Like the crook of your beloved's neck.

There is a spruce cone. There are many. When I hold it, when I run my fingers over its dry open wings, they play a tune that sounds like rain. *Do you know that each cone is a thumb piano in flower?*

There is a tangle of fishing line on the forest floor, a small clump the size of a tennis ball. If I blur my vision it appears the same colour as the spruce needles heaped against a tree. Close up, it is a mixture of orange, white and faded blue plastic threads – light tones in a dark wood. I wonder if the birds brought it here as nesting material? A bright orange strand hangs in the lowest branch of a spruce, about a metre off the ground. A tiny bird – a wren? – darts through the portal it makes with the neighbouring tree.

There is this tidal river. Here it meets the sea; empties out its secrets from a steep-sided sandy channel pricked with shipwrecks, followed up for clues by oystercatchers and curlews. The herons stand in wait. Later the water floods back in, bringing tidings of twigs, the shells of small crabs and surprisingly little plastic.

Whatever the tide, the herons keep watching, and waiting. In the long stillness of the hunt, there is a movement quick as knives. But if they fail to catch their prey, there is no bluster. They are back, poised, in an instant.

Beside and under and above this tidal river, there is earth and there is sky. Here, bridging earth and sky, there is the spruce. In the crown of that spruce is a nest. Two nests. Three. At the feet of that spruce is me. What is this place where time and matters mingle, where fish swim backwards into hungry mouths, crabs die in a field, a river flows upstream? My fingers glide through fallen needles, and twigs flecked with shit. A zen garden the width of my arms is forming around the boulder of me. From above, my dark-haired scalp is at the centre, extended limbs like featherless wings. Axis mundi: this tree that gives, and creaks in the wind.

*

A small body swings gently like a wind chime, high up in the spruce. Delicate trident claws point downwards and at awkward angles all at once. The chick hangs in a criss-cross of twigs, neck hooked over a branch; snagged at the intersection of one life and another. He, or she, must have been dead for a day or two. Rain-beaten feathers are grubby, the white ones almost as dark as the grey. Rigor mortis has fixed the beak slightly open, as if this heron was protesting gravity itself, as life was taken suddenly – *crick … crack* – mid-fall. From the forest floor, the whole suspended drama is silhouetted against an overcast sky. This small life, held still for a long moment in death, is leaned into by the straight dark torsos of spruce trunks. I follow the tall tree-lines to their vanishing point: the high white sky. The canopy sways and froths in the wind.

*

Now I spend whole days with them because this is where I can function without fear. And over time, they have learned not to fear me. It is as if they have learned that writing is my craft. They see me with notebook and pen bearing witness to the world with words, and they continue with their commutes of hunt and feed. I have decamped to the woods, made a desk from a discarded pallet, and in spite of myself, opened my laptop here under the trees. At the moment, I am not even writing *about* them. Finally I have some paid work. I am writing about an artist in Orkney who has devoted herself to living by the sea. She wanted to live with the briny truth of it and what it brings in its tides. Behind her house is one of the only dense clusters of trees in the archipelago. Exotic birds, blown off course, fly into her studio – an unexpected refuge mid-migration. She wishes to live at the shore even though hers is a bellwether island, flat and low and most vulnerable to sea level rise, even though it's certain her house will be taken by it. She knows she is at the end of a line, and she sees it as a privilege.

After some weeks in the woods, somehow hidden in plain sight only metres from the heronry, I found a hammock made from a scrap of fishing net strung between two short and gnarly oaks at the very edge of the riverbank. It has become my resting place. Suspended there, when my work is done, or coffee drunk, or lunch eaten, this is the place that I can just exist with them, not looking *at* them, not needing anything from them. I am beginning to know in my body their rhythms of hunt and flight and screech and click as the tide rises, and falls, in the estuary beside me.

One day, looking up into the dazzling green of the young oak leaves, the mesh of the hammock pressing into my back, I feel a presence land beside me. I turn my head slowly and slightly, to find Heron there, an arm's length away. I know that if I look head on she will leave. So I look with my peripheral vision. Our eyes are at the same height from the ground. I feel her, gauge her eye line meeting mine. Heron, too, looks at me sideways. We stay like this, expanding into each other's presence, for a long time. Or perhaps it is only a minute: I do not know, and it does not matter. I am no longer counting, or counting on, anything. I learn that looking is not the only way to see.

*

As summer unfurls, I realise that almost every day for three months I have been keeping company with these birds, and this small patch of forest a five-metre radius from their guano-flecked tree homes. I have watched the windblown lime green spruce shoots lose their colour and become yellow, then brown, and flatten. A rare and terrible circumstance has allowed this intimacy. It is a gift that has come in strange packaging. With my senses I have travelled vast distances, though my movements have become incrementally smaller, covering less terrain, as I home in to watch the truths and questions unfold in this pungent community of birds at the tip of a peninsula. Perception is fractal. It reveals itself the more you commit.

I notice the man-made noises return, layered and frequent. The banging of house building across the estuary. The boats out. The whine of a chainsaw; two. It must come as a shock for this year's herons, who were born into unprecedented silence. The absence of fossil-fuel-powered machines for a time was a revelation for me, as it was for many. In place of the roar of them, joining the birdsong were the subtle whispers of foot crunch, secateur snip, finger pluck, water splash. The cricket-like sound of my bicycle freewheeling. But humans have a propensity to change things; to move around quickly, and far. What would I learn, what would I create if I stayed only in a spruce forest for months, and had nothing to do but exist? When would I begin to smell like the forest? Does the forest smell me as I smell it?

*

It is nearly Midsummer, and tonight I am staying out. As I approached the wood this evening, three herons were perched on outer branches hanging over a little bay beside the river. They took off seawards and they're yet to return. The night is still and warm. I am down on the flat ground below the hammock with the pallet for a bedside table. I want to hear the herons as they go to sleep – *if* they go to sleep; to be with them as they make the first feed of dawn. The spruce needles carpeting the forest floor are dry and soft to lie on. Midges roam the landscape of my face, thirsting on my breath. The sea is calm and the silence is so total I can hear a ringing in my ears. A whisper of a breeze up by the hammock and now coming off the sea finds my face; relieves me of the midges for a while.

My eyes can just make out the silhouettes of the trees. The straight, tall regularity of their trunks play with my depth of field: which are near and which are far? A trail of resin running down the nearest tree paints a luminous 'I' into the gloom, the last bright thing besides the sky. The canopy blurs in a smudge of dark, the latticework of branches filtering out the remaining light, blue twilight draining to grey.

The gloaming heightens my sense of sound. I close my eyes. An oystercatcher pipes. A flutter of wings above – one of the little egrets, neighbours to the herons, rearranging itself in the nest? Now the rooks. Now my sleeping bag as I shuffle about for my sound recorder – I cannot help myself. How to keep a memory of this loud silence? A *splosh* in the river. A thumping rustle makes me open my eyes; a dark blob hops. A frog?

Through this briefest of nights, a few distant heron screeches echo in the moist, still air above the river. Have I slept at all? Have they? Behind my head, I notice a brightness through my eyelids. I open my eyes, roll them back, and find the sky is now blushing pale lemon. A dawn chorus slowly begins: oystercatchers more frequent now. A curlew. A cow lowing. A rodent scurrying in the nearby bracken. The first hoarse screech of a heron above me. Soon the first rook takes off, followed a few seconds later by a black explosion – *caaaaaw* – from the rookery. A wood pigeon makes a considered awakening.

3.30am. I get out of my sleeping bag and move to a spot beside the river. I sit on a rock above the high tide mark, watching and waiting. A bank of scurvy grass and thrift descends abruptly into mud and seaweed. Suddenly, I sense salt in the air. Is the tide rising?

The three hunting herons stalk the opposite bank but they disappear at the sight of me. In the nests above, the young herons and the little egrets are awakening – *awak awak ok ok ok ok ok neagh oooooo ok o kok.*

Thick mist rolls off the merse like a blanket of fleece, tumbling thinly over a sharp curve of the dawn-glowing river like carded wool. As the sun climbs higher in the sky the river becomes a silver snake, mist drifting on towards the sea as if it is its destiny – vapour united with ocean, water drawn to water. The air cools.

*

What is this place that can hold everything? The music of the awkward angles, the rising tides, the broken shells. What is this place that makes room for whatever I bring – makes humus of it, makes me human again?

I return here – to the spruce at my back, to the herons circling a raucous sky-crown, to the needles swimming my fingertips – as if my life depends on it; as if life itself depends on it. Each morning after pacing my rooms like a trapped animal, I find the courage to leave, and I get past the threshold of the red brick gatepost via new routes found out of necessity: up the hill behind that man's bungalow and down through the field of curious cows. Or I scramble down the mudbank of the river onto the floodplain, where I find the crab apple tree snagged with fleece and shelter in the shade of it. Where I find crab shells in the grass, washed up in the high tide mark with tidings of rushes.

With each step I take, further from that locus of fear, the air blooms, my pulse slows, my movements soften, until I am here with this place and these creatures: this raucous, insistent, feathered and winged ongoingness. This place that can hold everything. In *this* place, I can travel deep and stay at home.

FOLLOWING BONE, LAND, AND LOVE

Leonie Charlton

CONASG – GORSE

Sunshine draws scents of gorse, broom, bluebells. Horse sweat and leather are in the mix too. I am on a ten-day trip from Loch Etive in Argyll to Spean Bridge in Lochaber, with my travelling companion Shuna, our horses George and Boli, and Border Collies Ben and Marram. We ride past The Point where the hillside drops almost sheer into Loch Etive below, and where three hollies grow. Several years ago, prompted by artist Tracey Emin's marriage to a stone, I wrote a poem about these trees.

I married a holly tree
on the eastern shore,
seduced by green intensity,
roots' slow sundering of rock,
angles of pleasure between granite.
I was drawn to his moss-ridden silver,
low smile, muscular reach of patience.

What if, instead, I'd married his sister,
there signalling to otters from her cliff,
seeing sun fall from ravens' tongues,
thriving in the lee of stone
on strokes of lichen and luck.

How would it be to take the slight of her wind-turned
wrist in my hand, feel her spines distress my hair.

I have been married for twenty-five years. Martin is a man
with an innate understanding of complexity, one who can think
from scratch, and who sees things afresh in ways which enable
him to embrace different ways of being in the world. Is it this
ability to question the status quo, I wonder, that has led him
to engage with regenerative farming in the way he has, experi-
menting with new ways of working with the hill where we've had
a farming tenancy since 1998? Unhappy with the overall health
of the land, he wants to see more species thriving – from soil
microbiome to invertebrates, to plant life, to birds and mam-
mals. A year from now he will have sold his flock of six hundred
Scottish Blackface sheep, and will be increasing his Luing cattle
numbers. Alongside the cattle herd he will be caring for a flock
of just fifty sheep, and as a fanatical wool-wearer himself, and
with our children being keen knitters, he plans to replace the
Blackface with a native wool breed.

On the hill we tenant there are the remains of shielings where
cattle would have been summered. One of these is called Lag
a'Bhainne, 'milk hollow'. It has felt increasingly problematic to
be participating in a system where one species is thriving at
the expense of many others. I refer to sheep; I also refer to the
exceptionalism of humans. There has been a balance of sorts on
the hill all these years, in that the Blackface sheep have done
well up there. They are hardy, with strong social structures and
connections to the land, and their own unique intelligences. Our
hearts will ache at the loss of them, but hopefully, in time, the
cattle can work their ecological wonders.

FIADH – DEER

It's mid-afternoon and swelteringly hot when we ride past the spot I call Stag. I look across for a glimpse of bone, the last of the stag I shot here three years ago.

Stag

The sea-loch is kicked bright by white horses. On the hill a stag nibbles at bog myrtle buds. It's January and he's been struggling for months; he's been watched since the bracken began to lean over, his sharp-hipped lameness noted. Today he's shivering in the sleet, his hooves sinking between tussocks of pale Molinia, hind quarters tucked and trembling. Later, lying curled like a calf amongst the birch trees, he's shot. A woodcock flights the shock and a man lays a blade against one open eye just to be sure. He snaps off a birch branch from overhead, places it across the stag, leaves him there to be stripped back to bone.

Soon a pale breadth of rib cage moons under the downy birches. No recovery for the stag, but return and renewal inside a cub-worn fox scraping her den, inside an eagle tracing the sky, in rain running off bones. All the while bracken readies to furl up through the beloved unsprung last of him.

Shuna and I are sitting in the sun on a stone bench beside a brightly painted red door. Antlers lean against the bothy's corrugated tin walls.

On the skyline is Blackcock Rock, a historic lekking site where black grouse used to have their communal courtship displays. They haven't been seen here for years. This spring, dawn after dawn, I heard the underground-water sounds of lekking blackcock from my bed. I went looking, and found a single blackcock displaying to a hen pheasant, watched on all the while by her nonchalant pheasant mate. His display was a stunning choreography of blue-black and white. I cried, and thought of endings, and of endlings.

Contract stalkers are hammering the deer across the loch on Meall Dearg, Beinn Mheadhonach, Alasdair, the deer stalker here, told us last night.

Willow down blows in all directions despite the northerly breeze. Sweaty saddle pads dry in the sun and horses drink cold water from buckets. Ben flickers hopeful eyes between my face and the birch twig on my lap. What does it all mean: antlers whitening in the sun; last night's new moon a hint in daytime sky; snipe drumming.

Shuna is interested in talking about endings, the necessity and beauty of endings for new beginnings. She is puzzled but compassionate around my silence. Despite the sunshine I go inside to light the fire. For the rest of that day we don't talk about endings.

I load the stove with logs.

CUTHAG – CUCKOO

Cuckoos have been calling all morning. We stop by the Narachan Burn, and the small stone building sitting under the granite slabs of the south face of Beinn nan Lus. Today, back in Taynuilt, is my friend John's burial day – close family only. It feels fitting to be here at the old schoolhouse, and church, where he shared with me stories of his ancestors who'd lived here, and facets of the Gaelic concept of dùthchas, such as connection to one's birthplace, and to the community of that place.

The Cuckoo Stone
In memory of John MacFarlane

After tea, and stories of twelve tiny north-facing pebbles,
we follow you to one of the immemorial cattle crossings
of Allt a'chomhlachaidh – 'stream of talking together'.

You turn to us in October sun, shelling memories
of the ice-music this burn makes in winter,

of the horse mushrooms that thrive by your hawthorn,
this one with its roots lifting like bones under thinning skin,

like the seams of quartz that course through The Cuckoo Stone:
hand-on-rock you say this was where folk came to sort their
    differences,

we see this is where hawks now come to leave rabbits' feet.
You talk of feuds unresolved, battles fought over there on the
    Daileag,

raise your walking pole to Tom a' Phiobaire, – 'the piper's knoll'
a Highlander can pick out the sound of pipes anywhere.

We keep quiet with faint hope,
your Dunlops squelch in the quivering bog.

I first came to Glen Kinglass when I was eighteen. I have an overall sense of being at home in Argyll, but the feeling I have in this glen is a specific sense of knowing, even of belonging; as someone who, like many modern-day humans, has moved home a lot, has a scattered family and no real sense of roots, I don't use that word lightly. Researcher and writer Brené Brown says belonging is the opposite of fitting in, belonging is when and where you can be most yourself. It's probably no coincidence that I also feel a deep spiritual connection to this place – the rocks, rivers, and trees speak more loudly to me here than anywhere else.

CAORA – SHEEP

A handful of sheep graze the green areas around the ruins of Acharn Farm. The sheep were taken off these hills thirty years ago, but there are a few from neighbouring Castles Estate and Glen Noe that are still hefted here. I think about the gather last week at home, and what I wrote in my notebook:

The shouts and swears of the gatherers roll down the hill towards me where I'm sitting above the only wild rose in Fishers Glen. The long-tailed tits fall quiet. Now there's whistling to the dogs which lands more softly in my body than the swearing. I can see sheep stalling up above the hill fence – I feel into heat, confusion, young lambs, milk and lanolin, dung, and adrenaline. I wonder if the sheep will go this year, if this will be the last marking gather we ever do.

I also wonder, as I have many times in the past year or so, if there's anything about the sheep that the hill will miss, who Martin will be without the sheep, and to what extent his sense of belonging is tied up with them.

Changes in upland agriculture, as with deer management, bring up strong feelings in individuals and communities. Places like the Cuckoo Stone, or its modern-day equivalents to help with conflict resolution, are needed more than ever to help navigate endings, beginnings, and the range of change between.

EACH – HORSE

Boli has reacted badly to the midges – his young face is swollen, eyes dull, flanks tucked. We take our time making a difficult decision; the night stopovers we have planned for the rest of the trip are all potential midge hotspots, the forecast is hot and still, and we opt for the horses' sake to take them home. We'll come back and finish the journey on foot.

There's a tension between the horses' up-beat homeward strides, and our own disappointment. It's a privilege travelling with horses, masters of movement and embodied communication. Sharing space with their highly attuned senses, and responses, is a good way to stay aware and awake. Horses are also excellent at resting. Our friend and riding teacher, Kate Sandel, speaks of horses and trees as having a different sense of time to us, of them living in 'the long tide'.

Lessons from a Fly Fisherman
You go to the horses differently

they look at you sideways-on
appraising with amber eyes
your new wait, mid-air pause

where you find them
in their own deep

ALLT – RIVER

Sunshine floats like oil on the River Kinglass as we follow it back to Loch Etive.

I imagine the salmon struggling in the warming water, their

numbers already on the edge. I recently asked an Argyll-based wild fisheries manager how he stays positive: *because there's a Scottish Greens minister in Holyrood; because changes are happening in the regulation of fish farms; because wild salmon are adaptable; because – even though they may not be on the west coast of Scotland for much longer – they will survive, they'll migrate north.*

Loch Etive
I remember the bad stuff

*but today it's sun
and seal breath*

*green hairstreak butterflies
mind-blowing on gorse*

BÒ – COW

As we walk, we sweat a lot, chat very little. We stop to take off our backpacks and drink from warm burns.

Towards the end of the day, we come across fresh cow dung – there's a herd of Luing cattle up here at Blackmount, and I think of Martin.

Opal
(twenty-four years)
Luing cattle follow you, bellowing their brindles and sheer reds up a hillside. The bull heaves: flanks measuring the gravity of each step. Muzzles run and cows call throat-water sounds. Hooves sink and bones lever this whole of hide and milk and muscle. Calves gather, surge forwards light in their eyes and feet. In a lull things happen: the bull raises his head and lets pheromones

pour across his gums; calves throw their weight at udders, come up white-mouthed, frothing. The air is raucous with trodden bog myrtle, fresh cow shit, sunshine. Clegs bite, I swat my skin, breathe it all in.

that way you look back at your cows
how your t-shirt pins your clavicles
makes me want to start all over

Despite all the mutual appreciation, love, and respect between Martin and I, some of the relational elements between us have gone through times of flux, and have sometimes felt formless, even homeless. Mythologist, storyteller, and wilderness guide Martin Shaw writes in *Smoke Hole*, 'I don't encourage disorder as a lifestyle choice, rather a skill set for when the wolf eats our horse and we are far from the village. Little of substance gets forged without pressure. Duress can birth ingenuity.'[7]

Shaw writes about the importance of staying nimble in the face of paradox, and how it 'often takes an *event* to leave surety'. However messy, we sometimes need to leave surety to welcome in something new, or to heal wounds rumbling in the personal or communal psyche. Conflicts – relational and environmental – are playing out in the world right now, inviting new ways of thinking, inquiring, and imagining, if we are to find a way through the challenges facing us.

What my long-term relationship has taught me is that multiple and apparently opposing truths co-exist; that exploring less simplistic, dualistic, and binary thinking holds possibilities for reaching a more compassionate understanding of complexity, and

7   Martin Shaw, *Smoke Hole: Looking to the Wild in the Time of the Spyglass,* Chelsea Green Publishing Co, 2021

for engaging in the challenges we face individually, communally, locally, and globally.

CÙ – DOG

A man is running up the hill towards us, Ben's beetling about, his lead loose on the ground. The man starts shouting, Ben starts barking. I shout out, 'It's okay, he's friendly.'

'It's not okay, he should be on a lead.' The man runs past waving his stick, still shouting.

I swear after him. The anger and upset pass, but I can't stop thinking about that man.

Fast forward a few weeks and a woman explains to me – cheeks flushed, tremor in her voice – what it's like to have a deep fear of dogs, a terror that takes over your whole body. I think again about that man and wish I could apologise. This anger, this misunderstanding – is it to do with fear, and trauma, and how animals – including us – behave when we feel threatened? Is it to do with communication and taking responsibility? Is it to do with love? I remember Assynt this Spring, where a terribly-wounded stag was seen on Quinag, and the land managers of the hill, the John Muir Trust, were – rightly or wrongly – blamed. Social media was savage, and JMT's deer-management policy slated, likened to an 'unleashed dog'.

BREAC – TROUT

We're beside Allt na Bà, downstream from the stone bridge and out of sight and sound of walkers. Willows and rowans are growing out of the banks beyond reach of browsing deer.

The dogs burrow into cool peat below an overhang. Shuna and I swim. It's a head-under day. The bedrock is an orangey pink and flickers with reflections from the water. We go to the head of the pool where water's rushing in, lie on our backs, let the flow carry us.

Ben has got a stick stuck between two large rocks downstream. I go to help him, then climb onto a pony-sized boulder in the middle of the Bà. I'm thinking about the PhD I began, looking at Scotland's 'deer question' – a long-standing conflict between deer numbers and land use practices – through creative writing. I'm wondering whether to go back to it after a six-month suspension period; I'd said I'd make my decision after this time away, after I'd asked the hills.

I'm meant to be listening, but dogs, people, endings, heat, walking, back packs, midges … How can I listen? How can I find the space?

I consider meditating, but watch brown trout instead – how, gilded in sunlight, they hang over their barely moving shadows.

Suddenly the river has my full attention: what I see is that the pool we were swimming in is only half the river, and a fin of volcanic rock – that I'd thought was the riverbank – splits the flow in two. My heart jolts the way it does when it bumps into meaning, and I understand that it doesn't matter which decision I make; either side rejoins the river, either side is full of sun and shade, infused with deer scat, purple moor grass, essence of tadpole.

The side we were swimming in is the darkest, the deepest. I want to get back in, wholeheartedly, with curiosity, and with joy. I've heard it said in horse-training circles that curiosity is the opposite of fear. I can be like the trout – balancing, facing upstream, scenting the source. I can change direction, remember to thrive on story, light, and change. I can be attentive, and learn from the deer, dogs, horses, fish, how to be more sensate.

I can dare to be awake.

ÒIGHEAG – DAMSELFLY

A spin of iridescent blue.

A sun dropping fast as we drink double gins at the Kingshouse Hotel in Glencoe. We're chatting to a couple from America, two women in their late sixties. I turn to one of them. *Do you mind me asking, are you two together?*

It's complicated, she answers, quick as a minnow. *I'm married.*

I want to ask them more, I want to ask them about complexity and pluralism, nuance and possibility, but my limbs feel suddenly heavy as if sleepwalking. I look beyond the women to a young stag in velvet grazing the lawn, and beyond him to the dropping sun.

CRITHEANN – ASPEN

Since setting off from Black Corries we've been tracking down shade. In this heat we're acutely aware of the lack of trees and are worried about the dogs. We eventually find a slight, solitary aspen growing by a burn. Nearby is a salt lick on the top of a post in the middle of parched, deer-trodden ground. We sit in sparse leaf-shade and look across a moor shimmering in a petroleum-like haze. Davy, the deer stalker on this estate, is currently fighting forest fires in Cannich, wildfires that will end up being Scotland's largest to date.

My head is pounding. We refill water bottles in yet another slow-flowing, tepid burn.

We camp by the remains of Taigh na Cruaiche, a house and byre with nettles growing around the derelict doorways, and remnants of green pasture in the middle of a sea of cotton grass. We enjoy a breeze that keeps the midges away, and views to skylines of summits, and closer in over Loch Laidon, where, on a spatter of islands, are bursts of rowan, alder, birch.

SEANGAN – ANT

There they go, a puckle of red hinds – still scruffy in the spring moult – scattering from the railway tracks.

During the short, crowded train journey from Rannoch Station to Corrour, I've been thinking about the narrow-headed ant, *Formica exsecta*, hanging on in only a few remaining places in Scotland; these include the pinewoods near Mar Lodge in the Cairngorms, where I've sat by their bristling anthills, and somewhere not far from here in the Black Wood of Rannoch. The worker ants live brief lives, the queens a staggering average of twenty-seven years. Last year I wrote this poem, imagining – with my human limitations – what it might be like to be the narrow-headed ant queen.

Formica Exsecta i)

Workers – our-Body our-Being. You bring me gifts bright as the wren's blink: circles of sunny disposition; of pine and birch and heather-hold; of stoicism; of survival; of shared sky. Your explorations hum notes of honeydew and collaboration. I am in awe of your shrewdness, your noticings of dust. I nod to your volition, your acid tenacities. We can be safe in the quiver of this woven home, under cap of nibbled heather and grass. You'll die and I'll carry your epic griefs, your epic joys, into new generations. They'll flow along narrow-headed paths that teem with will.

Formica Exsecta ii)

I am Winter's Ant, curled inside resinous lengths of halfDark-halfLight, quiet beneath press of snow. I am mighty articulations of queendom, horizons of presence. I am at rest. I bear the scars of intervention: have been dug and turned over; have been caught, barrowed, exiled. Like all my kind I have focus. I aim. I. Am. I am queen of between; I reign over the light that gets through the cracks. I am free-choice and dawn-struck wings. I rest now so that I can strive and reach and aim. Again and again. So that my wings – those fierce opacities – may raise me to my mate, my mates, in thick summer air. I am passion. I am pine-besotted, needling, flickering. I am survival aroused. I am the crackle of polyamory. I am sun-spilt and sun-shared amongst wee-est, feistiest limbs. I tremble to the tune of eternity. I outlive, outwit, outshine. I radiate wings and sunlove. I shape eggs. I am queen, ruler of new colonies, integrator of genius. I am winter's antidote to shadow.

The train slows, stops, sheds people onto the platform at Corrour. The buzz of voices and Velcro, dig of walking poles into loose chippings, is electric.

CAORANN – ROWAN

Tonight, the dogs choose to sleep outside. They're hard to tell apart from the lichen-covered rocks scattered in the heather, but they're the warm-blooded ones, the ones with softer lines. There is a Gaelic word, milis, meaning 'sweet', also used to describe the soft lines of a living creature on the hill.

A single deer turns up and is barked away. Corrour Estate follows a strict deer cull, and she's the first hind we've seen. Here, on the next-to-last day of our trip, we see rowan saplings – the 'flying rowans' growing out of rocks beyond reach of deer which we've seen throughout the trip – but also rowans coming straight up through heather and blaeberry. Rowan trees are linked in Gaelic mythology with new beginnings, thresholds between worlds, and protection against dark forces. They're happy to grow alone, and also – rather than forming rowan woods – they prefer to grow alongside other species. Symbolically, they seem as resonant now as they have ever been. These rowan saplings in front of us are bright-leaved, glossy with dew. Immanent.

So many new beginnings from so many bloody endings.

A train comes through at dusk, headstrong and rhythmic. Wind and temperature drop, mist comes in and obscures the moon. We pull sleeping bags tight over our heads.

SEILCHEAG – SLUG

We wake to the calls and songs of greenshank, red grouse, skylark. We walk up Beinn na Lap, the Dappled Hill, and at 2,624ft sit down by the flowers of Mountain Everlasting. At 3,066ft the summit's insects drive us away. Back down at 2,952ft a pair of ptarmigans wait for us to be gone.

Back on the train, in the swaying press of bodies, I think again about narrow-headed ants, how they share warmth from the sun amongst themselves. How might it be if all these overheated humans, in this carriage, and out in the wider inflamed world, could cooperate for the common good of the generations coming down the line.

I look at the care-worn, sweaty tableau of faces around me, and after this time of walking, of being in the hills, I find myself strangely, fiercely, in love with humanity.

The last few walking-miles are on the A82's hot tarmac from Fort William, to where we left the horse box and pick-up two weeks before. In the steady stream of traffic, a hearse passes us, slow and black, shiny as a slug on the dawn hill. A look of understanding passes between Shuna and I – *Whatever it takes, let's be awake.*

Let's be awake to our feet, our hearts, to the aches and the joys, as we head back to our respective homes, back towards different hills and their herds of cattle, horses, deer, their endings and beginnings, and towards everything growing between.

FROM SUNDAY SCHOOL TO SALEM, MASS:

One Witch's Pilgrimage

Claire Askew

Before I left for Salem, Massachusetts, I made three offerings to take with me. Each was a small parcel, about the size of a walnut. The offerings contained thyme (to recognise courage), lavender (for devotion), rosemary (for its purifying properties), rosehips (for love), cloves (for the relief of pain) and white rose petals (for innocence). I wrapped each bundle in a handwritten message: the first read *thank you for your courage and legacy*, the second *you were heroes*, and the third – the message that felt most vital – *I'm sorry for what was done to you*. It was October 2019. I'd read Stacy Schiff's 2015 book *The Witches: Salem 1692, A History* three times. My copy felt like an artefact – a holy book, of sorts – spine-bent, dog-eared and underlined. The Salem witch trials constituted a mass tragedy that occurred 294 years before I was born. They led to twenty politically motivated murders, the events that preceded them snarled up in ideas around gender, race, class, propriety, property and nationhood. As well as the twenty people executed, dozens more were persecuted, tortured, imprisoned, and/or killed by the conditions of their incarceration. The youngest was Mercy Good, who was born and died in the Salem jail – the daughter of the accused Sarah Good. The oldest was Giles Corey, tortured to death at the age of eighty-one. I'd known of the Salem witch trials all my life, having grown up with the 1993 Disney film *Hocus Pocus* and read Arthur Miller's *The Crucible* in high school. Now I was flying over three thousand miles to do … well, something. To leave an offering. To try and find somewhere to put my own useless and belated rage.

*

The spiritual background of my life was and is Anglican. I was baptised into the Protestant Anglican church and taken to Sunday services throughout my childhood. After my family moved to Scotland when I was nine, we continued to attend Church of England services, driving over the border every week to the Church of St Gregory The Great in the wild and lonely hamlet of Kirknewton, Northumberland. At twelve, I took confirmation classes in the nearby town of Wooler, and was confirmed in St Mary's Church, Wooler by the Bishop of Newcastle. I wore a blue velvet dress and a gold cross my godparents had gifted to me. I was asked to choose a hymn for the congregation to sing, and chose 'Hills Of The North Rejoice',[8] because it had always felt like a hymn about the place I was from. The lyrics are primarily about calling Christians in every corner of the world to worship, but as a teenager I liked the fact that this hymn celebrated "river and mountain spring … valley and lowland." At that age, I was almost always outside, and knew in some deep, unconscious way that the hills and trees I climbed and the rivers I swam in were holy places. The music was the main reason I liked church. I sang in the choir, and mostly daydreamed through the readings and sermon and Nicene Creed, waiting for the next hymn.

Unfortunately for my parents and my confirmation classmates

8 'Hills Of The North Rejoice' was composed by Charles Oakley (1832–65).

and the Bishop of Newcastle, I began to get interested in witches at around this time. I was vaguely aware of the family legend that we Askews were related to a woman who'd been burned at the stake. This was the late 1990s, and a pop culture witch craze was being manufactured and aggressively sold to tween and teen girls and young women. After *Hocus Pocus* came *The Craft* in 1996, followed by *Practical Magic* in 1998. My school's library was full of R.L. Stine's *Goosebumps* books and Jill Murphy's *The Worst Witch* series. Buying myself a purple notebook and calling it my Book of Shadows felt practically mandatory. It wasn't until my mother found my little collection of pressed leaves and scribbled "spells" that I became aware of a tension between thinking of oneself as a witch and continuing to attend church. Somehow – whether by my mother's hand or my own, I can't quite remember – my little Book of Shadows ended up being put in the stove.

*

I don't think it's unfair to say that Salem is a Disney theme park of a town that thrives under capitalism. Had I been raised Catholic, I might have been better prepared for this element of my trip, as Catholic sites of pilgrimage are usually also places where the pilgrim can buy saint candles and medals, beads and ikons, ostensibly as a donation to the upkeep of the holy site, but also as a form of proof to take home – something to say *look, I got there, I did it*. Protestants in general don't get to collect talismans – a thing I've always been a little jealous about, as I find Catholic iconography very beautiful.

One of the first things I did upon arriving in Salem was head to the Witch Museum, housed in a former church built in the 1840s. The museum has excellent intentions: its website states, "the mission of this organization is to be the voice to the innocent victims of witch-hunts, from 1692 to the present day. By interpreting this history ... we strive to bring awareness to the endurance of scape-goating and injustice." My visit, though, felt aggressively managed: I was aware that I was, ultimately, being slowly funnelled towards the extensive gift shop. Later, as I wandered the streets of Salem, I had the opportunity to buy basically any witch-themed item I liked. Some stores offered sweatshop tat: t-shirts that read *100% That Witch*; bumper stickers declaring *My other car is a broom* or *Yes I can drive a stick*. At the other end of the spectrum were small businesses selling one-of-a-kind artisan broomsticks, limited edition incense blends, bespoke blown glass scrying balls. Everywhere, there were candles: scented candles, candles with intentions, blessings or hexes baked into them, candles upon candles upon candles. Images of Sarah, Mary and Winifred Sanderson were far more in evidence in downtown Salem than any of the accused "witches" of the 1692 trials.

I wasn't turning my nose up at this: the opportunity to buy quirky witch-adjacent tchotchkes was part of the reason I'd made the trip. But alongside the dollars I'd budgeted for souvenirs, the three offerings I'd brought with me felt heavy in my pocket. I longed for a church, an altar, or a statue. The town's most famous and prominent statue depicts a fictional character: Samantha Stephens of the 1960s sitcom *Bewitched*, played by Elizabeth Montgomery. Erected in 2005, the statue feels like a bizarre decision for a place literally built on the site of a tragedy. Contemporary Salem is a disconcertingly make-believe place: a theme park haunted house ride on top of a mass grave.

*

I had quietly folded away my interest in witches for almost twenty years, though I dressed as a witch every Halloween and stayed a die-hard fan of goth-adjacent witchy women like Kate Bush, Tori Amos and the duo Shakespears Sister. It wasn't until my early thirties that I took a proper interest in that old family story and discovered who the woman burned at the stake really was. She wasn't, it turned out, a witch: Anne Askew was a Protestant martyr, born in Lincolnshire in 1521 and forced to marry nobleman Thomas Kyme after her sister Martha – Kyme's original betrothed – died unexpectedly. Anne was a political protester and, I'd argue, an early advocate for women's rights. After her marriage she continued to call herself Askew and became one of the first English women to petition for a divorce, claiming Kyme was abusive. Her petition was, perhaps unsurprisingly, refused.

Anne found solace in her Protestant faith, though she soon attracted negative attention among the English nobility for her outspoken views. She objected to the barriers that prevented her from worshipping as she wished, staging a protest by sitting in Lincoln Cathedral for a full week and reading the Great Bible there – something women were prohibited from doing. Eventually, Anne was arrested and imprisoned in the Tower of London. At the time, Henry VIII's court was eager to forge an alliance with the Roman Catholic Emperor Charles V, which led to what we might now call a witch hunt, of sorts. Traditionalists in Henry's court hoped to weed out the devout Protestants among their peers, and saw the outspoken Anne as a useful source of information. Anne was subjected to torture by racking, in the hope that she'd name other members of the nobility[9] who "believed as she did." She refused to be broken, and said nothing under torture. As a result, she was burned at the stake on charges of heresy on July 16th 1546 at Smithfield, London. She was twenty-five.

9   Their particular hope was that Anne might name the then queen, Catherine Parr.

Learning about Anne made me very proud, but also incredibly angry. I became angrier still when my reading about the wider socio-political context of her life led me to the two-hundred-year witchcraft hysteria[10] that swept Europe between around 1550 and 1750: two centuries of panicked eugenics, during which individuals – mostly, though not exclusively, women – were put to death for, in summary, failing to live up to the prescribed social mores of the time. A non-exhaustive list of grounds for execution included falling ill, being disabled, exhibiting mental health problems, falling pregnant, failing to fall pregnant, having sex, not having sex, failing to marry, being poor, asking for help, taking care of animals, and entering into property disputes.

I read about Ursley Kemp, executed in Chelmsford, Essex in 1582 after her interlocutors coerced "testimony" out of her eight-year-old son. I read about the 1727 trial of Janet Horne[11] and her daughter, which went ahead though Horne was likely suffering from dementia, and her daughter was physically disabled. Though some of those accused worked with herbal medicine or dabbled in what's now called folk magic, none of them were actually attending sabbats, flying through the air or partaking in the ritual murder of babies, as the witch-hunters suggested. Not only was Anne Askew not a witch, but none of these so-called 'witches' were, either.

10 It's been suggested to me that I ought not to call it a 'hysteria,' in light of the negative feminine stereotypes that exist around this word. I'd argue that this period of history saw a definitive hysteria perpetrated almost exclusively by men, i.e. a perfect example we can point to when we're told it's woman who are the hysterical ones.

11 Janet (or Jenny) Horne was a placeholder name given to many accused witches in the north of Scotland during this time: the real names of both victims went unrecorded. Though the younger woman escaped, her mother was burned at the stake after being tarred and paraded through the Sutherland town of Dornoch.

*

I eventually found the sacred site I was looking for. The Proctor's Ledge memorial is relatively new, dedicated by the mayor of Salem in July 2017, 325 years to the day after the first five Salem women were executed. It's a twenty-minute walk from the throng of downtown, the route initially making its way through streets of Greek Revival and Italianate houses hung with Halloween decorations for the tourists. After a while, though, I found myself walking among parking garages and auto-repair lots, the nondescript industrial terrain of Anytown, USA. I checked my Google Maps a lot, worried I was going the wrong way, dismayed by the lack of signage pointing me towards this important historical site. I'd expected to be walking among other pilgrims, but the closer I got to Proctor's Ledge, the more alone I became. I remembered as I crossed the 107, a four-lane trunk road that runs along the north shore of Massachusetts, that most of America isn't built for pedestrians. Finally – and to my great relief – I found the memorial site hidden away in a small residential street, round the back of a Walgreens. The low, semi-circular stone wall is set into the base of the hill where the nineteen Salem witch trial hangings took place. At the time I visited, it wasn't signposted, and not a soul was there to see me as I laid two of my three offerings into gaps between the scrubbed grey stones.

It felt right that this place was so quiet: creating a space for reflection of this type would be borderline impossible amid the hubbub of Essex Street with its black pointy hats and pillaged white sage. It also wasn't lost on me that the memorial was built like an altar: stone, with a flat top where other people had already laid flowers, coins, candles, scribbled pieces of paper. Perhaps most importantly, this was the place – the actual place – where what happened, happened. This was the site of nineteen out of those twenty murders, and the place where at least some of the remains of those nineteen individuals were buried in an unmarked grave. *This* place had that feeling I was looking for: the feeling I'd experienced before in churches and cathedrals and graveyards. This place knew, somehow, in its bones, that what had happened here was not the stuff of creaky horror movies or Halloween hijinks. I was standing on the site of a mass tragedy, and the land itself remembered.

Salem wasn't like other witch trials: it is less a story of a community deciding how to deal with the individuals it perceives as outliers, and more a story of a community ensuring its own survival by partially eating itself. Though it was largely forgotten for a time, Salem now occupies a rather lurid place in the popular collective imagination, mostly thanks to *The Crucible*, Arthur Miller's 1953 play. Though Miller insisted that *The Crucible* 'is taken from history', he played a central role in transforming – as Stacy Schiff puts it – 'a story of women in peril into one about perilous women.' The Salem trials hinged around the 'testimony' of a group of young women whose ages ranged from nine to twenty. One by one, the girls fell victim to mystery afflictions they claimed were demonic in nature: they suffered convulsions, screamed, barked like dogs and reported being pushed and pinched by unseen hands. These girls named individuals in Salem they believed were working with the Devil to create these torments, and as a result of their testimony, twenty people were murdered.

The temptation when thinking, talking or writing about the trials is to jump to the obvious question: what, if you'll pardon the pun, *possessed* these girls? Over the years, a variety of theories have been put forward, from teenage boredom to mass hysteria to convulsive ergotism, a type of food poisoning caused by a fungus that grows on grain. Did these accusers know what they were doing? Did they realise they were going to cause untold suffering? Did they understand what they were doing was wrong? Did they feel guilty afterwards? What, exactly, *happened* here? Standing at the Proctor's Ledge memorial, I realised I couldn't hear that chorus of chattering, convulsing girls. I wasn't thinking about *The Crucible* or *Bewitched* or *Hocus Pocus*. I was glad to have found a physical place where I could be still and think of the people whose stories ought, by rights, to be central when we think or talk or write about Salem.

*

The longer I've lived, and the more I've read about the not-witches of the past, the more 'witchy' I have become. I'd lived in Edinburgh for fifteen years by the time I booked my trip to Salem, and although I loved the city with its narrow closes and crow-stepped roofs, I found myself yearning for wild places. I'd started reading about herbalism, astronomy and astrology, Tarot and British folk customs. I was angry with the church of the past for what it had colluded in, caused and done. Almost all the witch trials I'd read about were full of the interlocutors' urgent righteousness, yet their machinations seemed utterly, depressingly *human*: nothing to do with God at all. I remembered then why I'd stopped attending church as an older teen: not because I rejected Christianity, but because its rituals had come to seem counterintuitive. Why were we sitting in a cold, dark room at the same prescribed time every week to talk and sing about the glory of God's creation, when said creation was *out there* to interact with – and by extension, rejoice in – every second of every day? Why were we letting a book written by politicians and bureaucrats centuries ago dictate how we communed with the divine? No one ever gave me a satisfactory answer.

Twenty years later, I realised I didn't need one: I could just start doing it, start celebrating the divine world in whatever way I pleased. I found myself using Tarot cards and thinking the process felt like prayer: I was sending my hope or confusion or despair or joy out into the universe, and receiving an answer. I found myself looking at an astronomical diagram of the orbit of Venus and thinking, "now *that* is holy." I found myself building little altars in my flat – altars not so much to God as to the world, to space, to weather, to the seasons, and really, wasn't that the same thing? I marked full moons and solstices but also Candlemas, Easter, and Lent. I sat at my Yule altar and sang *Gabriel's Message*, a Basque folk carol and my all-time favourite piece of religious music. I was learning to worship in a way that felt truly holy to me, the way nothing ever had before. I was becoming a contradiction: a Christian witch.

But where does a Christian witch go to make herself a sacred space? To this day, I have a soft spot for churches, but I prefer to be in them alone. Anglican churches offer a very specific sensory experience: they're usually cold, and very quiet, and they smell of decaying flowers and damp plaster and dust. I like to potter around in a church, completely alone, talking to God in my head or out loud, reading the inscriptions on the memorial plaques. As part of a congregation, I feel I can worship, but I can't *commune*. I can rejoice and give thanks, but I can't effectively rage, despair, or – crucially – listen. I learned fairly quickly that I'm what other witches some-times call *a solitary*. For me, aloneness is next to godliness.

*

I found I was particularly struck by one of the Salem victim's sto-ries: that of Giles Corey, one of seven men murdered during the trials, and the only person executed at Salem whose name isn't included on the Proctor's Ledge memorial. Accused of witchcraft along with his wife Martha, Giles refused to enter a plea. He knew that those who entered no plea could not be tried. He may also have known it was possible that he'd be executed, and in that event the state could not seize his property from his surviving family if he hadn't pled guilty or not guilty. Determined to extract a plea, Sheriff George Corwin ordered that Giles Corey be tortured. The eighty-one-year-old was placed, naked, into a pit, and covered with a board, onto which huge stones were laid. The idea was to force Giles into a plea so he could then be put on trial. However, Giles remained steadfast – the story goes that he shouted "more weight!" as the stones were piled onto him. He was crushed to death on September 17th 1692.

Giles Corey's death is often not counted among the official tally of those executed at Salem, and I had mixed feelings about his absence from Proctor's Ledge. Supposedly, his death by crushing was accidental, though of course, had he survived to be taken to trial, the likelihood is that he would have been murdered anyway, as his wife Martha was. I admit that Proctor's Ledge probably isn't the right place to commemorate Giles: it isn't the site of his death, and his remains aren't there. They are somewhere else in Salem, though upsettingly no one knows quite where: he was buried in an unmarked grave and the location never accurately recorded. It's believed his remains are somewhere on the land where the town's Howard Street cemetery now stands. That was where I headed to with the last of my three offerings, the one I'd saved specifically for Giles Corey: *I'm sorry for what was done to you.* I wandered the fenced confines of the grassy cemetery for a long time, hating the fact that Giles still hadn't received what the other nineteen eventually had: a specific, meaningful place for reflection. Howard Street is close to Salem Common where, in October at least, a fairground is erected for the tourists. As I stood thinking about Giles, deliberating over where to leave my little offering, I could smell the hot fat from the donut fryers and hear the distant screams of children riding in waltzers and bumper cars. In the end, I chose to leave my handful of well-travelled herbs and petals in the hollow of an old elm that stood near the centre of the cemetery's chain-linked plot. I'd read that an elm's roots can spread out further than the tree is tall. My hope was that somehow, wherever on this piece of land he was, Giles might be reached by the message.

*

I refer to my trip to Salem as a pilgrimage, the religious connotations of that word not lost on me. It felt like a happy accident that I ended up in a place of such intense contradiction at precisely the time I was embracing my own contradictory notions of faith and identity. Salem's consumerist, haunted house elements unsettled the traditionally raised Christian in me. The angry part of me wasn't sure how the fancy brooms and rubber bats and endless candles were connected to the suffering of the many people persecuted here: those people were, after all, the very reason Salem is known as Witch City. But the longer I thought about it, the more I realised that even the paper ghosts and pumpkins on the stoops of Salem's houses were trying to mean something. As Sarah Marshall notes, "[we] have a hard time finding language or emotions to describe to ourselves this space around mass tragedy, and just the concept of a place being haunted – I feel like that's another way of calling something sacred, or showing respect for the dead."[12] The witch in me was able to find a place amid the fairground noise and Christian graves to leave her not-quite-secular, not-quite-religious offerings. Perhaps all of Salem is an altar to the people who suffered and died to build it?

12 Sarah Marshall – journalist, horror movie enthusiast and host of the podcast *You're Wrong About* – was talking to Jamie Loftus as part of the *You're Wrong About* episode on self-proclaimed ghost-hunters Ed and Lorraine Warren, released on 8th November 2021.

*

Shortly after I returned from Salem, the Covid-19 pandemic brought the world to a terrifying standstill. Cooped up in my shared Edinburgh flat, taking my precious state-sanctioned walk along the footpaths of Inverleith Park once each day, I had a lot of time to reflect on what I'd learned from my visit to Witch City. I spent a lot more time than I ever had before doing what I call ritual observances: marking Sabbats and saints' days, following the phases of the moon. In April 2020 I turned my entire room into a Beltane altar with bunches of flowers, candles, incense wafting from my tenement window. I journaled a lot, and the journal entries read like a frightened person trying to bargain with God. I made an ever-expanding list of the things I'd do once lockdowns lifted, and the longer the list went on, the more I realised that most things on it were to do with being outside, alone, in wild spaces. In the summer of 2020, restrictions eased just enough for me to abandon my cramped Edinburgh flat and begin a gradual relocation. By the spring of 2021, I'd moved myself and all my possessions to a tiny Georgian cottage in Northern Cumbria, a house with a working farm behind it, song thrushes and bats in the trees. From here, I could make my way to wild places without breaking the restrictions that were still in force. I visited Mayburgh Henge and Long Meg and her Daughters, little-known neolithic stone circles which felt, to me, like outdoor churches. I climbed the long track to Bowscale Tarn – a body of water said to contain two giant, ancient fish named Adam and Eve – and swam alone in its clear, icy water.

I sought, and found, aloneness that felt sacred: a place to talk to God and the land and whatever else might be listening about my fear, my anger, my despair. Now, a big part of my practice as a Christian witch involves noticing as often as I can my desire to exert dominion over other beings, as the church once did over ordinary, marginalised people. I notice the shudder I feel when I come across a spider in my house – the weird, primal desire to destroy it – and force myself to remember how large I am, how much power I hold over this tiny life. I no longer put spiders out into the garden, knowing as I always have that they'll most likely die of cold. Instead, I relocate them to the dusty cavity under my bath, which means I see them more often and have to endure the shudder, but also that we coexist in peace. The spiders remind me I am large, and powerful, but I can choose to be either harmful or benign. Swimming in a cold Cumbrian tarn reminds me I am small, and vulnerable, but I can choose to be either cautious or brave. In the times I manage to be both brave and benign, I think about God, and Anne Askew, and the 'witches' of old. I go to 'church' as often as I can, to rejoice in the hills of the North.

BLEEDING MONT BLANC

Anna Fleming

On the glacier. Fresh snow, dazzling light, new tracks across the stage. A chough flits and circles, ever-curious, looking for food. From the ice, ancient red granite rises in spires and needles, rumbling now as grit is released down the mountain. Meanwhile a small orange butterfly floats up the rock-face, moving from one green alpine cushion to another.

My first summer in the Alps and every morning there is a set dance in Chamonix. Ropes and axes swing from the bags of alpinists racing across town – pausing in the boulangerie queue for croissant and baguette – then onwards to the station. Nod to the lift operators then pile into the crowded cable-car, and up! Flying over alpine trees and flowers, ears popping with the altitude while the cables wind into the cooling air.

We step out at the Aiguille du Midi. An odd sensation. Lightheaded, slight breathlessness. No trees and few plants. Just granite, ice and creaking infrastructure. Through the dripping tunnels, we avoid looking at the cables, wires, spikes and pitons holding the lift station together. A messy assemblage. It is said that when they built the station, they poured concrete in to fill the gaps between the rocks, and the concrete sloughed out again further down the mountain.

This place feels unstable and yet hordes of people come up every day. We weave through tourists dressed in t-shirts and jeans, women with handbags and heels, marvelling at the scenery, thrilled by the otherworldliness of this high-altitude pagoda, some seeming a little lost, as though they are not entirely sure what they're doing up here.

Our purpose is clearer. We jump over the locked gate and stop in the ice cave to gear up for the crossing. The cave is bigger now than it was a few weeks ago. It opens out every day in the summer heat like the heart of a gigantic frozen flower.

We step out of the tunnel, crampons biting into the snow, lose our breath again, just for a moment. There's the panorama. The Mont Blanc Massif. An upland of peaks and needles – the aiguilles – sharpened by time into rough red spires emerging from oceans of ice.

My first summer in the Alps and many days are spent like this, rushing up into the heights.

*

On this day we are out late, our plans in disarray. Snow came down overnight, thick and heavy across the tops, burying our previous notion – to drive from Chamonix to Switzerland and climb the Eiger. We mope around town, anxious for a new scheme to emerge.

The officials in the Office de Haute Montaigne have no news. "Beaucoup de neige." Come back after lunch.

We're drifting, wandering, killing time. Passing flash clothing shops of Swiss watches and high-end brands. Climbing shops filled with racks and racks of colourful pricey equipment. Runners in little shorts lapping the town. Buskers playing for quick cash. People sitting outside the cafés and restaurants, some working on laptops, others talking, idling over a relaxed lunch with partner, friends or family. The world comes to Chamonix, they say.

At 3pm, we return to the Office de Haute Montaigne. Up the stairs into the room in the rafters holding maps and information, even a little book where you can sign your name, put your mobile number and appeal for climbing partners. An office reminiscent of another time, when information was housed in physical buildings and extracted from reluctant officials – rather than the dizzying platforms of the infinite online.

I go to the desk, taking my questions to a youngish official. Dressed for activity, he exudes professional ennui.

"Parlez-vous anglais?"

"Yes, a little," he responds.

I want to know how much snow there is higher up and whether we can climb a certain peak tomorrow. With the language barrier, I keep my enquiry simple. As direct as the French.

"Can we climb Mont Blanc?" I ask.

"By what route?"

"The Trois Monts."

A beautiful route – a fine long outing. Never desperately difficult, the Trois Monts would offer us a journey through epic high-altitude scenery passing over two glaciated mountains before reaching the final icon, Mont Blanc itself. Since the Eiger was off, this seemed a fitting conclusion to my time in Chamonix.

"Yes," he answers. "You can climb it this way," then with a slight smile: "If you like avalanche."

*

After the snow arête, we cross the glacier and head up the slopes towards Refuge des Cosmiques. At 3,613m altitude, it is the base for climbing Mont Blanc. Like the Aiguille du Midi, it is another striking structure of glass, metal and timber, perched on the rocks over the Vallée Blanche. Crampons come off and we clang up the metal staircase, leaving the light, stamping snow from our feet and heading into the dark vestibule. The boot room is busy: many ropes and bags hanging from hooks, shoes neatly lined up underneath. We find a corner with some pegs and boxes and stash our kit, then join the queue at reception.

The Guardian looks up from her chart. "Mont Blanc?" she asks.

Mont Blanc. Mont Blanc. That question again. This time a simple answer.

"No. Not Mont Blanc."

We are still undecided about what we will do tomorrow. The avalanche risk has pushed Mont Blanc away from its leading position and instead we have conjured a range of options – many schemes and ideas – that could pass the time in the Massif. While the future is unclear, at this moment, we have a particular reason to avoid using the giant's name.

"Well then what will you do?"

A range of possibilities – we list and obfuscate – maybe a rock climb – a long walk over the glacier – perhaps a cable-car ride into Italy for coffee? The guardian nods, satisfied.

"Ok, 4am. Room 7: Destivelle. Breakfast at 4."

Success. In this place, the name Mont Blanc assigns you a bed in the 1am room. The hour is unthinkable. Perhaps we are naïve, but neither of us feels that this long snowy walk deserves such an outrageous start.

*

The sun passes over to the west and a cool silence fills the snow peaks. Most climbers are down now – back to the valley – or nestled in their stopping place.

Inside the refuge, some sixty of us sit on benches in the dining room, talking over this and that, hunting for familiar faces.

Conversations in four, five or six languages, always circling back to the same line. Where are you from? What will you climb? What will the next day hold? An air of anticipation charges the room. Like a run of salmon, we are waiting in the pool, braced for the leap.

The Polish group have been placed in the 1am room. Theirs is a tough job. The first to climb the Trois Monts for some days, they will be breaking trail in the fresh snow, wading through deep powder all the way to the last top.

I excuse myself and go to the bathroom.

An unpleasant scene. One room for all genders and the sort of smell that encourages you to do your business swiftly. I select a cubicle, lock the door and hover over the drop. Then wipe. And there it is.

A pink streak on the tissue. Les Anglais ont debarqué.

There was no sign down in the valley but now we're here, sure enough, Bloody Mary comes visiting.

Did I have something? Yes. Downstairs. At the last minute, I had put my mooncup in my rucksack: a half-thought, just-in-case gesture. I didn't really know where my cycle was at – the rhythm was off. The mountains had pulled it off kilter. With all the activity, my cycle had shortened, the crimson flow coming more often.

I drop the sheet into the pit. No flush on the toilet. No water in the taps. Liquid arrives in these heights in plastic bottles, flown in by helicopter and sold for eye-watering prices.

Suddenly, the mooncup, my simple reliable period companion in its sweet little draw-string bag; my mooncup, the dependable one, the one you empty, rinse and use again – the sustainable friendly option – seemed impossible.

In a place where every drop of water counts, what is there for the blood? How to rinse Mother Nature? At the hand santiser, a vision floats before me. A mooncup emptied on the glacier: blood-red on snow-white mountain. Lady Macbeth with blood on her hands. No good. It was no good. I had to find something else. But what?

Back to the dining room, I scan the tables. A sea of men. Bearded men, shaved men, young men, old men. Men speaking French, English, Polish, Italian and Spanish. Men in expensive jackets; scruffy climbers in grubby old t-shirts full of holes. Bankers, dirt-bags, guides – every class of men – but no one looking like they might carry the essential kit.

They say gender equality is moving through the mountains – with more girls and women travelling everywhere – but this refuge is still a man's world. I'm stranded: lost without the sister-hood. Where are the women?

There. Behind the bar, helping the kitchen-men to serve the evening meal.

I walk over, weaving through the tables, playing it cool while aiming for the Guardian, hoping she can help.

"Excusez-moi, j'ai un problème."

"Oui?"

I lean in close, blushing at this pressing moment. A teenager again, I'm uncomfortable and ashamed, caught desperately off guard.

"I … umm," I lean in closer with a desire to whisper, mumbling the word 'period' in English.

"Ah," she says. "Come with me."

Behind the counter, through the kitchen and into the tiny reception space, she reaches out to the wooden shelves and brings down boxes of tampons and pads, ready and open.

"Take what you need," she says.

I could kiss her.

"It's nothing," she says, as I fill my pockets.

"You have some job."

"Yes. We cook, we clean, we wake through the night for breakfast. I look after the staff and the visitors. Sometimes," she confides, "I feel like superwoman."

In my eyes, she is a goddess.

Back through the kitchen and file out across the dining room, calmer now, floating on waves of relief.

Then someone grabs my arm.

"Excuse me? You dropped something?" In his hand, a shiny gold plastic wrapper. One of my precious little tampons.

"Merci."

I zip my pockets closed.

*

After dinner, the room falls quiet and the Guardian climbs onto a chair to address the congregation.

"I will read you the weather forecast. First en français, then in English."

Silence. Anticipation. All eyes on her, wondering what the next day will hold.

The French is well received: people break into smiles, chattering and murmuring as she progresses to the English and then concludes, proclaiming for the entire room:

"So you see, you have your forecast. You can climb Mont Blanc."

Cheers, applause, grins from all!

C and I turn to each other, excited as children. Every other scheme vanishes – blown away by her simple report. We have her blessing. Tomorrow we will climb Mont Blanc.

*

The sun sinks lower. Wings of ice spread across the windows. The mountains, falling into shadow, turn blue. Only Mont Blanc, the last top, the highest point in western Europe, has the sun. Always last to hold the light, the huge round dome briefly turns pink.

Salmon, now fading, soon lilac and then into serene blue as the peak drops back into shadow and night falls across the Massif.

Blue, black and icy. Temperature drops, darkness all around. On beds of rock or shining ice, climbers shiver through the night while stars and satellites circle overhead. Fleeting tranquillity: soon the first headlamps are out, the early risers ascending their routes, climbing through the night towards the warming day.

Why here, now? Why Mont Blanc? Why climb? It was 1786 when the first climbers in wool and linen, leather and iron moved up through the icefields on a quest. A Genevan had offered a prize: a generous financial reward for the first person to reach the lofty summit! His curiosity was boundless. A man of science, practiced through mind and body, out in the field and up in the mountains, restless for knowledge. Botany, glaciology, geology, physics, astronomy, the chemistry of the atmosphere – he even made a device to measure the blueness of the sky.

And soon after those first men, the first woman. In 1808, Marie Paradis, struggling for air at the top but still showing from the outset that women can! And since that time, so many more pilgrims of every age, gender and nationality have walked this way, pacing through the snows, for glory or conquest, magic and madness. But how many menstruating on the mountain, I wonder? There is no record of women's secret afflictions, no accounts in the journals and diaries of our red river flowing in the heights. Perhaps we came down, or didn't go? Or simply got on with it, dealing with the pain and shame in our own way, with secret asides to trusted companions and grumbles and growls, the feminine version of the stiff upper lip.

Collective visions, dreams of hope, fear and desire ... in our beds in the waiting room we drift through the night, in and out of sleep. Heart rate elevated, body working to get enough air, struggling to rest, until surely, inevitably...

4am. The alarm sounds, cutting through the night.

*

Waves of ice rise ahead and we wade through the snow, one foot in front of another, axe in hand, zigzagging from darkness to daybreak.

Step, breathe, step, breathe. Sunrise approaching, rosy on the horizon. Keep walking, up through the snow, always one foot in front of the other, finding our way into the rhythm of the mountain day. The breath harder to catch as we move uphill, lungs and muscles protesting slightly, but still, keep moving at a good pace, flowing up the mountain.

Now a steep step, a ladder-like line of footprints running up through the snow.

I swing the pick of the axe into the snow, find the biting point and pull up. Calves awake and burning in protest at this steep section, but the pain will not last. Soon at the top, and walking again, up, up, along the glacier: keep moving, keep the pace, keep breathing.

All day in the snow. A glaring white expanse that burns eyes and skin. A blank page. A cloud space. An ocean frozen white. And now the Mer de Glace melting away – the sea of ice turned into a sad little bed of rocks. From the heights, the mountain guides and glaciologists issue warning after warning. Rapid loss: accelerating warming. Rocks falling. Permafrost melting. Catastrophic changes. The safe limits for humanity – passed. The world entering a dangerous new unknown. Hard truths to take in, in this place of extreme beauty.

Higher on the glacier, a cleft yawns open. A crevasse, newly widened, the jaws grotesque and yellow with rotten snow. Yet something oddly appealing is here: a desire to lean in, a wish to comprehend the space of sacred air held within the old blue ice. The sculptural chasm, a cathedral within the glacier.

Scottish artist Wilhelmina Barns-Graham was transfixed by the holes in the ice. Visiting Grindelwald in 1949 sparked an epiphany in her mind. Back in her studio, she worked and worked at the forms, transforming the ice into abstraction. Her work shows a restless eye, a shifting perspective that could be the artist or the ice itself – or both perhaps, acting together. Some of her paintings show water pooling on the surface, or lines of accumulation, like the rings in a tree. Others take the glacier as a wider whole with sweeping lines, triangles, circles and other shapes in blue and white, brown and black. An animate geometry springs from the canvas.

The artwork is intense: a close focus and carefully considered experimental methodology. Some paintings: monstrous! The glacier has bones, fractures, decay. Others suggest genesis. In Glacier Crystal, an ovoid sits under the ice. An egg? The kernel of new life?

Then, a lurch in my stomach. Nausea and a deep-seated inner ache, sharpening sometimes to a cramp. My womb on the move. Hand on my belly, nursing my body, hoping it will pass. Strange how the pain comes from within each month. The woman's gift: the cost of new life.

Onwards, under the seracs. Wondrous blue-white cliffs made up of magical layers and layers of snow, compacted into blue lines, patterned like the bedding planes of sandstone. Each line a past winter: a faithful record of each year's snow accumulation. And now with the melt, the account shows only loss. How can somewhere so tough, so dangerous, also feel so fragile?

A whistling of anxiety tells me not to linger here.

*

A labyrinth of serac and crevasse, footprints winding through the glacial interior, all churned up and opening apart, then up a little more, and there. The summit shoulder of Mont Blanc du Tacul. The first peak of the Trois Monts.

Heart pounds – we stop to breathe – space for exhilaration – lifted in the wonder of being sky high.

Two air balloons rise from the north, and in no time they have gained serious elevation. Flying south – passing over this mountain chain – astonishing – over Mont Maudit, racing into Italy. Absurd to think of the little people up there, so tiny in the big sky over the vast mountains, holding the sides of their little basket while it hurtles some five thousand metres up in the sky.

The balloons soon vanish, alerting us to something else. The wind is strong: much stronger than we had thought it would be. And the sky is clouding over. The weather is not as rosy as the hut Guardian had led us to believe.

No matter. We pick up and continue around to the second peak. Mont Maudit. The Cursed Mountain. On these treacherous slopes, the blue-sky dream fades. We cross insecure slabs, moving as fast as we can, keen to leave this section behind. Maudit disappears into a cloud. Footprints are disappearing. The wind shifts the snow, redistributing the powder across the slopes, filling in each step. It is hard work, plunging my feet into this soft mass, breaking fresh trail.

Then a steep icy slope. The technical crux of our day. This is the hardest bit of climbing on the whole route with the steepest section of snow, requiring good, precise use of axe, crampons and balance. Beneath the soft white powder lies the hard, unforgiving blue ice falling away into the great abyss … one slip now and a swift return to the ocean of the unborn.

*

Two men appear out of the cloud, descending from the third summit.

"How is it?" I ask.

English is not their first language – they are Italian, perhaps. Their response is simple and direct.

"Very cold. Much colder than here. And windier. You need to be very strong to keep going."

We check in and discuss. C is OK: I am OK. The situation is not ideal but once we stop and breathe neither feels desperately out of comfort zone. C has worked in Antarctica – his body is familiar with snow and storms – and he moves with the assurance of someone who knows the mountains.

For me, this is the highest I have climbed, but as we stand here in the storm, memories course through my veins. Snowdonia, the Lake District, Scotland: the various high points of our little island. Mountains in wind, rain and snow. Blizzard and white-out. No path. No signs. No footprints. Cold. Intimidation. Disorientation. Comparing this moment with these past sensations, a curious sense of security begins to creep in, despite it all.

As we continue around the mountain, circling towards a distant white dome, I am surprised to find a new strength powering my limbs. The knowledge that my body has met situations like this before. Knowing that I can continue armed with a ruggedness that has been whipped into me by the same processes that shape the battered pines at the entrance to the Cairngorm plateau.

*

Every step a challenge … lungs working hard, laboured breath, sucking air out of the atmosphere, even as the wind whips it away. I no longer feel my period. The pain has gone – subsumed into everything else that my body is doing. I remember wryly some advice written onto the packaging of the sanitary pads I used as a teenager: light exercise can relieve the symptoms of menstrual cramping.

Sound of spindrift – grains of snow and ice flying across the surface like sand over a dune. The wind buffeting, pushing us around, tearing at the fabric of my synthetic clothing, buzzing and roaring, flapping in great agitation. Another layer on; thick gloves; a fight to keep moving uphill.

The summit dome beckoning ahead, clouds hurtling across the top.

Somewhere on these slopes – a rush, a wet flow in my knickers and the tampon has reached capacity. Blood oozing into my knickers, the body following its course. No matter.

Part of the skies now, we enter a lenticular cloud. I love these clouds, have loved watching them drift high in the sky over the Cairngorms and Yorkshire Dales, curved by the contours of air and mountain. But up here, inside the cloud, all is savage. Shards of ice whip our skin, wind battering the body, burning the senses raw.

Zig: zag. Numb. Gasping up the mountain, following a line trodden in by boots and crampons, metal points biting into the white.

Zig: zag. On the zigs, we fly. No gravity, no altitude, the wind thrusting us up the incline. On the zags, we battle. Every step against the current, forcing our way through the blast accelerating around the mountain.

Each zag a horror. Breath snatched, the air already so thin. Ice whipping the face. On the corners, we meet and huddle together like penguins, gasping for a moment of comfort, then proceed through the storm, jackets flapping, beating loud as loose sails.

C tries to explain – a meteorologist – a keen knowledge of wind and conditions from forecasting in Antarctica, but I struggle to catch his drift – my mind floating out – something about localised conditions – the ground heightening the wind – a sharpening around the edge …

Seventy metres from the top, three German men stop. The guide and his clients left the refuge with us: they have made it this far, but no further. The situation is too much. They descend. We continue.

*

Zig: zag, keep moving, keep breathing, and then, a levelling. Nothing much. A flat bit of snow and no more uphill.

We made it?

A wind-battered … top? Europe? Monte Bianco? Hallowed heights, still white and gleaming.

Breathe. Keep breathing. Pace along the flattening and realise: this is it.

A summit seen and unseen by thousands of eyes before me, ice storm abating, senses numbed … raw-blasted by the mountain … a dizzying feeling, sensing the African plate pushing into this continent, thrusting up these rocks, the entire arc of the Alps, a rainbow mountain-chain curving across Southern Europe.

C and I pause. Photos and food. The summit and the food: difficult to stomach – the body still reeling from its journey into the heights. How many women have stood here, I wonder, bleeding on Mont Blanc before me? How many more to come, armed with tampons and crampons, pads, cups and axes, following the salty-iron pilgrim's path, hiding their secret shame?

And now we're here, at the frozen apex of this wonder in the sky, I feel the ground wobbling, uncertain. A melting at my feet. Sun pushing heat into the crystals. A new energy in the mountain: snow failing to linger, ice melting, glacier coming apart, rocks collapse.

Strange to reach the peak of Europe and find this deep vulnerability, a fragility that runs through life and land, uniting us all. One truth. Strikingly simple but mysteriously hard to see.

The mountain herself is bleeding out.

REWRITING THE HERO'S JOURNEY

Lee Craigie

Across the world, the power of storytelling has helped carve out the value systems by which communities of people choose to live. For thousands of years we have listened to heroic stories of adventurous men conquering our natural landscapes. The risks they have taken and the suffering they have endured have landed them atop lofty pedestals and offered a narrative that we have only recently started to question. When we do pause a moment to consider the values this way of being perpetuates, we often find egotistical ambition and single-mindedness at the core of many of these great achievements. But what would our world feel like if, instead, we found inspiration in the everyday and the ordinary? What if, instead of stories of overcoming near-death in hostile environments, we celebrated a person's intuition and their ability to notice detail and remain in the moment? What if, rather than conquering a natural landscape, our protagonist paused with humility and awe to consider their place in the global scheme of things, placing wider outcomes before personal ego? Would this avoidance of heroic drama be well received?

Well, let's see …

In the world of endurance bike racing, participants travel as fast as possible while remaining entirely self-supported over a set distance of hundreds – or sometimes thousands – of miles. The stories that are shared at the end of these long rides (in hostels, campsites, pubs and cafés) are what creates such a close-knit and connected community – one which I am honoured and humbled to be part of. Yet even in my community, the stories of near misses, equipment failure and the general overcoming of adversity are what grab people's attention and sometimes even media headlines. Over time, I've noticed that the people who tell these stories are the gregarious, outgoing riders. There is hand waving and eye widening, vein popping and superlative dropping, all of which captivates audiences who are wowed by accounts of risk-taking, impressed by the stoic bandaging of gaping wounds and in awe of the ingenious fixing of catastrophic mechanical bike failures.

But what of those riders who seem to have suffered no more than the most manageable of saddle sores, who sailed with minimum effort and maximum grace through the same weather, terrain and distances as their louder companions? These people sit more quietly around the fire or at the bar and take up only a fraction of the space their hand-waving counterparts do, because their stories don't grab attention with the same shocking force. In these untold stories that are brim-full of patience, kindness and gratitude, no one gets struck by lightning because no one was reckless enough to be out in adverse weather conditions in the first place. No one flew over any handlebars and had to splint their own femur because those people had been riding that difficult descent within their skill level. No one suffered from hypothermia because, despite not achieving an arbitrary milage on one dark, cold night, the choice to find shelter and make use of the warm, dry equipment carried for the purpose seemed obvious.

We see attention drawn to the extreme and the dramatic everywhere: in politics, in business, in sport, on social media. But we don't seem able to see through these glorified stories of derring-do to the parallel, underpinning sub-plots of stubbornness, selfish desire and destructive progress.

And so, after a career of full-time mountain bike racing, I felt compelled to stop and consider whether my life-long passion was now serving me. Only when I took this step back from the intense focus on timed laps and on beating others over a finish line did I find the space to remember the reason I fell in love with riding bikes in the first place: I had always loved the journey.

It would have been easy for me to draw a line under racing and return to using my bike strictly for recreation, but in polarising these two ways of moving by bike I risked losing the nuance of it all. Racing doesn't have to be inherently selfish and egotistical. Recreational riding isn't automatically joyful. Like in everything we undertake, if we pause to interrogate our intentions, to investigate *how* we want to be rather that *what* we want to achieve, then we come closer to the art of living an authentic, fulfilled existence. When a group of people share a common goal and agree to operate under the same code of conduct in order to pursue it, purpose and possibility open up. By turning away from racing entirely, I would be missing an opportunity to practise a different way of being in amongst the pressures and stresses that can mirror those present in our everyday lives.

There is a race called Further Elements that takes place around the Highlands of Scotland. The route is long and arduous and crosses some extremely challenging landscapes, a long way from towns or cities. Images that promote the event show athletic men in Lycra clothing, leaning into the wind and rain while battling over torrenting rivers and high cols – so perhaps it's unsurprising that in 2023, the gender ratio of participants was four women to fifty men. The route started and finished at Corrour Station, a concrete railway platform plopped on the edge of the bleak and foreboding Rannoch Moor. It comprised 500km of B-roads, old military roads, historic drove roads and technical single-track descents from high mountain passes. It was scheduled for the end of October, so the weather would most likely offer extremes of temperature, wind speed and precipitation and, as always, the clock would not stop for sleeping and eating or for mechanical or bodily failure.

These kind of events are where it is hardest, and therefore most meaningful, to practise a different way of travelling by bike. My friends and I have begun to notice that the expectations of what it takes to sign up to such a challenge never involve humility and patience, but rather physical strength and single-minded focus. We decided to challenge those long-standing narratives by prioritising fun and camaraderie instead.

Philippa, Alice and I are three women who naturally share this ethos and who ride at a similar speed to one another. Our friendship was born of a shared love of wild places and our innate need to experience them in vital, sharp relief, something that comes more easily to us when travelling long distances and stripped of our everyday comforts and familiarities. We tune in to our surroundings and each other in order to thrive, not just survive, when the going inevitably gets tough. Doing so together has always consolidated our reverence for the natural world, with the added benefit of deepening our mutual care for each other. For this reason we are usually drawn to the sorts of events that take us through mountainous terrain and rely on more than just physical prowess.

Further Elements is not a high-profile event driven by corporate sponsorship, but the brain child of an artist and friend, Camille McMillan. His routes often involve seemingly arbitrary detours and additional challenges that make no sense to those wishing to complete a fast linear journey, but which make perfect sense to those with a curious mind and a sense of adventure. Camille is fascinated by landscape and how history has changed how we experience the world we move through. His routes are all personally researched, usually with a nod to those who used them in days gone by and the purpose the old roads used to serve. We decided that our little team would travel Camille's route[13] together, not racing but supporting and encouraging each other instead. It was with this deliberate intention that we set off in the wind and rain from Corrour.

For centuries the Scottish Highlands has been a bastion of traditional hunting, shooting and fishing estates. This has led to claims that Scotland has the most unequal land ownership in Europe. Commercial farming and monocrop forestry plantations have further depleted our landscapes. But there is now a shift of focus away from traditional, extractive practices towards the regeneration of Scotland's depleted native woodland in order to promote biodiversity, slow climate change and provide a range of fairly paid employment possibilities across rural Scotland. So it seemed fitting that our journey would begin and end on the Corrour Estate – a stronghold of this new wave of land steward-ship, informed by approaches closely aligned to our own.

We began our ride early in the morning on the estate's fast, wide gravel tracks. The sun remained shy behind dense cloud cover, sheets of light rain ruffling the surface of Loch Ossian as we rode east, in one large homogenous pack, towards Laggan. Riders then swung north to Kingussie and past Ruthven Barracks, a monu-ment that has stood for hundreds of years to remind us of our unfortunate leanings towards war and oppression. In Glen Feshie I realised that each time I am here I hear, see and smell more. Thanks to our happier leanings towards healing and regeneration, the Glen is getting louder with bird song and the once scraggly birch now clings a little less fearfully to strengthened riverbanks. The weak sun had by now struggled free and we were delighted by

---

13 The full route can be viewed on Komoot: tinyurl.com/mpbrydfa

a brief rainbow over the vibrant thickets of young oak, alder and rowan trees. But that would be the last of our weather fortune. By the time a complex series of old military and drove roads delivered us to the inaccessible village of Tomintoul, the sky had long since darkened and the rain had started in cruel torrents.

It's easy to follow these off-road routes and consider yourself pioneering, but riding them mindfully allows the time to reflect on the reasons they came into existence in the first place. By moving on foot or bike we are brought closer to the travellers of earlier times who used to walk with their cattle and other tradable wares. Riding an old drove road reunites me with the natural rhythms my ancestors must have been buoyed by, and I can never help but compare their essential, meaningful and – possibly – more satisfying tasks with my own arbitrary recreational objectives for travelling along these historic highways.

It was getting dark by the time we stopped for dinner at the pub in Tomintoul. We sat wide-eyed in damp clothes, listening to the rain driving off the windows and dreading the long, exposed traverse over the Northern Cairngorms to Ballater where we planned to stop for the night. Outside, the lights of other riders passed by the pub and disappeared into the gathering darkness. We ordered pints of beer and waited a little longer in the warmth of the bar, then cajoled each other to get stiffly to our feet again and back outside. This high, windswept section over Loch Builig would be a test.

The persistent rain fell in torrents swelling the River Avon and all its tributaries, making our progress slow and treacherous. We waded through rivers up to our thighs and, once on the other side of each crossing, pedalled fast to warm up again. We passed riders who had frozen to the spot with trepidation at crossing these rivers alone, and one unfortunate soul who had punctured his skinny rear tyre and was running the remaining thirty kilometres to Ballater, carrying his bike. We stopped to offer him help but he was intent on remaining self-supported, so we rode away glancing backwards from time to time to watch his headlight retreating in the growing distance between us. The rain didn't let up.

It was very late by the time we reached Ballater and we were saturated and very cold. We dropped our bikes under cover of the local bike shop veranda, meaning to sleep in its relative shelter, then went to the pub again to warm up. It was here, pressed up against radiators and nursing cups of hot chocolate, that a kind B&B owner overheard our story and insisted we stay with him free of charge. This type of chance encounter only happens when you are open to it, and all three of us were more than happy to take him up on his generous offer of warm beds and a tumble drier.

I have lost count of the number of times strangers have offered me help or refuge on long bike journeys. I think that travelling by bicycle strips back the barriers between rider and the natural world and acts as a conduit between people too. A compassionate soul who spots someone journeying by bike often makes the assumption that the traveller might be hungry, tired, cold or lost. This is often true, and the lack of barriers makes it easier for help to be offered and accepted. I am always surprised and delighted by how much both parties seem to get from this kind of exchange, and it makes me mindful of the generosity of spirit it requires to accept help as well as to offer it. As a female bike rider who regularly travels solo, I am often asked if I don't feel vulnerable travelling alone and my answer is always: "Of course I do! That's the point!" Vulnerability is not a trait we like to associate ourselves with for fear of exploitation, and we spend a great deal of energy attempting to hide it. But in my experience, as long as you trust your own judgment of a situation then sharing something of your true self is a gift for both giver and receiver. It's worth asking the question: what do I stand to lose by NOT opening myself up to this opportunity for connection?

The next morning dawned cold and grey, but our stiff bodies were revived by donning dry clothes and enjoying breakfast at a local café. While we ate, other riders emerged, still wet from uncomfortable nights spent in bivvy bags in the rain, the whites of their eyes betraying just how hard they were having to work to keep themselves together emotionally. By contrast we felt lucky and buoyed by our chance encounter with our philanthropic B&B owner, and we left Ballater with bodies, minds and bikes in good working order. The ride over the Capel Mounth was brutally steep, cold and very windy. Low cloud covered the plateau we were inching towards. But there is a picture of us near the top, together with our friend Michal who had joined us by this point – we are wearing wide grins, our hoods up against the wind and rain, our spirits obviously high.

We rode on, descending into the Angus glens on tricky single tracks, then out to Alyth on tarmac road into a strong, bitingly cold headwind. We had each other in sight, moderating our speed to stay within reach of one another and casting glances over shoulders to ensure we were all okay. Another detour to yet another pub regrouped us as we drank whisky in the afternoon to make the flooded road ride towards Dunkeld feel more manageable. We caught up with two men hunched over their handlebars and battling to keep their bikes moving forward. It was clear from their bedraggled appearance that they hadn't stopped to dry off and restore their morale, but when we overtook them they put on a burst of speed to regain the lead. We let them ride off, out of their saddles, straining into the wind to keep an advantage that we didn't want.

The instinct to ignore our most basic of needs and deny ourselves any comfort is often synonymous with endurance sport. We are told that we must push through discomfort and resist giving in to our vulnerabilities. Being strong appears to mean denying ourselves what we need. It's true that giving in to every distraction of the mind or each new bodily discomfort will make completing an endurance challenge very hard, but an intimate knowledge of oneself means that differentiating between needs and wants is much easier. In a recent 1000km race across the Balkans, Alice messaged me with this very dilemma. It was day one of seven. It had rained relentlessly and she had covered one hundred and twenty hilly kilometres already. At only 7pm her racing instinct was an insistent voice in her head telling her to keep moving into the dark night. A storm was forecast and she knew that carrying on would mean a cold, damp, late night with only a bivvy bag for shelter. In another part of her mind, a more primal instinct was tugging at her, preventing her from mindlessly carrying on with her ride.

We messaged back and forth about how she was feeling and what she was thinking, and eventually Alice decided that checking into a hotel, prioritising warmth and food and letting the race go ahead of her, would help her enjoy the ride in the days to come. She battled briefly with the idea that this might make her – one of only two women undertaking the challenge – look weak or pathetic in a pack of strong men. She then regained perspective and listened to her bodily wisdom. Alice woke early the next day and set off from her refuge in dry conditions with a newly oiled chain and a full stomach. She was in eightieth position. Over the next six days she steadily climbed through the pack of male riders who had pushed on that first night and depleted themselves in the harsh conditions. Alice continued to ride within herself and six days later finished strong in ninth place overall. She had successfully negotiated all that social conditioning to do the right thing for her body and mind, and it had worked.

In our Scottish journey, after 250km of wet and windy riding, we stopped at an Indian restaurant to take care of ourselves. We were tired but elated and it didn't feel too difficult to put on our wet clothes over full stomachs and continue on our shared journey that evening. Up and over another high pass and onto a ridge-line in complete darkness, our lights bouncing off the low cloud that entirely enveloped us now. The starless sky and open moorland merged into the same featureless entity. It was just us, our breathing and the woody late season heather catching our tyres. It felt like the most privileged of things, to be pushing pedals with strong, healthy bodies on a dirty autumn night when everyone else was insulated against the elements in the valley far below us. After an invigorating, slippy descent into Comrie accompanied by whoops of exhilaration we slept a second night in an Airbnb belonging to a friend. We knew this was not in the spirit of the event, when up ahead tired riders were huddled under bridges or in outbuildings to escape the rain. But for us, like in Alice's Trans-Balkan experience, shelter meant that the next morning we could ride fresh again: we knew that we weren't going to be the first riders back to Corrour, but we were going to make it back intact in body and soul.

We inched northwards, sharing what food we had left and pausing to help one another with any technical problems that were starting to emerge. A reroute due to a dangerous bridge meant a boggy trot though some woodland, but we were distracted from any discomfort by the vibrant greens of the mosses and the evening sunlight catching off swollen raindrops that lingered on the autumnal leaves. This type of grateful noticing is the biggest gift a ride like this can offer, if (as with benevolent strangers who want to help the vulnerable traveller) we can be open and curious enough to let the gift be given and received. When we eventually gained the final pass above Rannoch Station, we regrouped one final time and helped each other negotiate the swollen river crossings in complete darkness. We rolled off the hillside and over the finish line side by side, dropping our bikes by the little wooden hostel building before collapsing in a big group hug.

In the busy restaurant attached to Corrour Station, broken, depleted men were sleeping, eating or sitting in small groups regaling each other with stories of their solo rides. Some riders had quit, others had crashed, and one person bragged he had stolen food in order to get to the finish line. Some riders had ignored the detour and prioritised speed to reach the finish. Some people were now sick and shivering, having ridden too long without sufficient food and warmth. One man had spent an hour trying to dislodge his bike from a river in spate and had, he claimed, feared for his life. The two riders who were first over the line in a staggeringly fast time had finished together, one of them following the other due to a navigational device failure.

Their stories were fascinating and well told, but had a hard edge to them that suggested pain and despair. Our ride had been completely different. We had completed the same route but felt like we had won a different sort of race. We had taken care of ourselves, of each other, and had moved with conscientious understanding of the terrain and the elements that threatened to derail our ride at every opportunity. We had ridden fast and well and had relied on our own skill, kit and equipment to complete the route – but we had not ridden alone or slept outside, and this was not how these races were intended to be ridden. We didn't care. We announced that we wanted to be disqualified from the race standings. This ride had not been a race to the bitter end for any of us. It had been a test of empathy, mutual care and respect for our surroundings. Despite – or perhaps because of – the weather, we had felt awe and gratitude for our freedom to move through wild places where our ancestors had travelled long before we began inventing con-voluted endurance challenges in order to feel connected to our bodies and the natural world. We had felt like we had been part of something much bigger than ourselves – not simply undertaking a shared challenge with a community of like-minded souls, but part of our landscape, our history, the complicated thrum of life in its most vital and primal state.

Camille, the race director, would not accept our disqualifica-tion. He insisted that Further Elements was an adventure within a set of ambiguous rules and that it was up to individuals to follow their own code of conduct. I think he valued the alternative nar-rative we were trying to build, and made the arbitrary point of jokingly disqualifying riders for not riding with a bell mounted on their handlebars (an item in his essential equipment list) in an attempt to subtly back up the subjective definition of a clean ride.

The following day we posted our story to social media, includ-ing details of our voluntary disqualification, and then watched with interest as the comments from online spectators flooded in. "Why would you enter a race and not race?" "Did you not feel you had undermined the spirit of the event by riding together?" "Why did you sleep inside and stop so often in pubs?" We didn't address these questions at the time. We preferred to leave these questions hanging in the air for others to reflect on and make their own judgements of. We were proud of what our ride had represented and unperturbed by such scrutiny. The pervading narratives of individual success and heroic suffering, we had realised, are so limiting. My friends and I choose to ride our bikes for the freedom it offers our bodies and minds. This had been our race and we felt we had completed it in the spirit of how we want to be in the world: a differently heroic tale, and one we could be proud of.

HOW FAR MY BODY CAN GO

Marjorie Lotfi

I.

A few years ago, I was the writer in residence at Coastworld, a literary festival on the east coast of Scotland. Many mornings that spring I woke early and, after dropping my children at school in Edinburgh, drove for an hour to Dunbar to walk the shores and harbour with a notebook. The twenty-six miles between my day-to-day life and the residency mattered; travelling that hour gave me time to work through any lingering worries I needed to deal with in my 'real life' so that when I arrived, my mind was clear to write.

Just as most people who travel will tell you that they aren't in control of the journey, most writers also aren't in charge of what they write. I might sit down to write about my grandmother, for example, and a story about a game of cards with my brother will emerge instead. What I wrote those mornings in Dunbar was no exception – not a story of my own or one linked to the rich history of the area, but that of a woman who wrote letters to the sea in winter. I'd wanted to write about other subjects, but when I tried, nothing would come after a line or two.

Eventually, I gave in and let the woman inhabit my notebook and imagination. Having written letters to the sea in my earliest poems, she surprised me one morning by deciding to walk into the water to deliver her words directly.

Winter reply

She writes a letter to the sea, loops
*   forms together as she's been taught*
to make language. It contains all and none
*   of the words she wants to speak.*
She's worried about tides, about her lines
*   returning while she's sleeping, afraid*
she'll wake in the morning to dog walkers
*   along the shore avoiding her eyes.*
She decides to deliver it herself, holds it between
*   two hands resting on her head, walks*
into the water, now moving ice; it's no matter
*   that she's forgotten how to swim.*

Because each act of writing is akin to departure for an unmapped journey, I didn't see this development coming. The question for me then was where to go next? I decided that I needed to act on the writing itself, take up the woman's story in body as well as in language. It was late February/early March, the time when the North Sea is at its coldest. For the next few trips, I surreptitiously packed towels and a hot water bottle into my boot and put on an extra fleece under my coat. I knew that if my children discovered what I was doing, they'd object, and even worse, they'd worry. I showed them the photos of the dark sea those stormy mornings, but never of myself in it.

For the first dip, I chose a spot to enter the water close to the car. The sum of my emergency plan was getting in my car and putting the heat on to warm up. I didn't tell anyone where I was going, didn't have an orange buoy or neoprene boots and gloves, things I now consider basics for exposing my body to cold water. Those mornings, I stripped to my swimming costume and simply walked into the sea, standing waist-deep for a few minutes, watching the horizon as an anchoring point before taking a quick plunge to the nape of my neck and getting out.

I don't remember learning to swim. We paddled in the Caspian Sea during the hottest days as children in Iran, with my mother under a shelter further up the sand, and also swam in my Aunt's deep swimming pool during our summers in Ohio, in both cases without floats or adults to help. I was a decent, if not fast swimmer; by the time I was out of primary school, I'd joined the local swim team and spent many summer mornings swimming endless laps of a pool before 9am. When I left school, I qualified as a lifeguard to earn some money in the summers between years at university.

I still regard myself as a reasonable swimmer, which meant that getting in the North Sea on those mornings in March didn't feel as foolish as it now seems in retrospect. After the first couple of dips, I read up on after-drop and the symptoms of hypothermia. That research gave me permission, in those forays into the sea, to pay close attention to how my body was responding to the cold and then the wind, to the changing depth of the sea as the tide moved around me. The fact that I persisted despite the dangers, only mitigating them where possible, is probably linked to the fact that I hadn't thought of *myself and my own safety* in many years, always putting the safety of others, especially my children, first. (I believed the biggest risk – should something terrible happen to me – was the impact that that event would have on them.)

Over a succession of dips, I found I was able to stay in longer than the panic that always set in in the first minute or two – that old fight or flight instinct – and longer than it took to remind my brain that I was not going to die. The more often I was able to get into the water and trust that I *was* able to stay, the shorter the periods of panic lasted. I slowly realised that I was stronger than I'd thought I was, and could often extend my stay a few seconds beyond what my brain assumed would be my breaking point. By the time the next poem arrived, placing my body in the water was making space for something new, something I didn't have a name for yet.

She is a woman who walks into the sea
  to ask her question, drops it like a pebble
from her pocket and watches it sink.
  All answers come from behind; if we could
simply catch our former selves,
  they'd show us where to look: beneath the belly
of a small whitecap, or in the water's draw
  against the pebbles, even in the curve
of seaweed deposited in strips of morse code
  on the shore. She is a woman who walks
into the sea. Today, the sea answers back
  in roars, as if tired with her regular descent
into its icy waters only to look out
  at the horizon, in the direction of home.

It's hard to overstate the impact that mothering can have on a woman's body and brain. Now that I'm older and edging towards the menopause, I understand that women of mothering age have hormones that allow us to set aside our own needs in preference to the needs of those around us. In my case, I was someone who wouldn't stop doing – actively *doing* – in order to be sure that the ship she was steering would stay afloat.

Other than those moments in the water, my life at that stage rarely, if ever, left me time to think. I was a mum of four children, working part time and taking care of the needs of countless other people; I spent all day every day (often right up to the moment I fell into bed) doing something useful. My four children attended three separate schools, all with different musical activities and feeding times, and although their father was around and helped when he could, he was working full time so the organisation and most of the day-to-day management of our lives fell to me. I also had a charity to co-direct as well as a fledgling freelance writing career. When my kids went to bed (*if* they went to bed), I started on prep for my workshops and did a final check-in on the charity. Every morning, I woke before the children did, usually at 6am, to get ahead on the day.

Looking back, it's not a wonder that getting in the sea was transformative. In the water, I couldn't think about the endless list of tasks still left to be done, or my family worries. Being in cold water, especially water in motion as it is on the Dunbar coast, makes you consider your own body with a primal urgency; cold water taught me that my strength was beyond my expectations, but also to consider myself first. Once I was in the water, the chitter of my daily life just disappeared. Suddenly *I* was there – not the sum of my accomplishments or activities, my hopes or plans, the identities imposed by others – not a brown foreigner or poet or mum of four – just the *me* of that very moment, a woman who walked into cold water beyond her ankles and stood still looking at the horizon.

If you'd asked me at any point during those years of early mothering what *I* wanted, I'd have answered in relation to the health and happiness of my children, or my wider family. I don't think I had a sense of what I was aiming for, except the other side of parenting: sending my children out into the world aware of their own abilities, including the ability to keep themselves safe, and an understanding of how to experience joy. Looking back now, I didn't apply that same standard to my own future, committing the classic mother's mistake of forgetting herself. As the children grew, even though they went to school during the day, their needs became more and more complex; rather than freeing me up for projects of my own, my life got smaller and smaller. I remember a neighbour asking me what my hobbies were, and I laughed before staring back at him blankly. I didn't know what to say, and certainly didn't know what I'd do with time if I'd had any to spare.

In the sea that spring, I didn't finally ask myself what I wanted; it wasn't as clear-cut as that. But I did stop in the water – while writing about a woman who walked into the water and often didn't walk out again – and then, a little beyond what I thought I could withstand, I walked back out to the sand, and warmed myself up, being as careful as could be in the circumstances. I created windows where I checked in with my body and began to ask myself – for the first time – if I was okay, possibly *because of* the women in my writing. And like so many other things in life – once you start asking the questions, you can't stop. Almost more importantly, you need to be prepared for the answers when they come.

I travelled back to that coastline water week after week, challenging myself to stay in a little longer, then to take more time for my writing, now completely engrossed in the project at hand. When banks of seaweed stood in my way, I didn't wallow in the shallows but waded right through them. I knew by then that if I could manage the initial cold of the water I could also walk in without knowing what was beneath my feet, and could even wait for my heart to stop skipping beats (which it did regularly, for unknown reasons) and then continue on into deeper water. *I can do hard things* became, and still is, my mantra, something I'd never had before.

Quiet or Quit
She is a woman who walks
into the sea, doesn't halt for tide
or kelp, its splayed fingers hiding
the serrated edges of stone.

She is a woman who walks
into the sea, though mussels stand
between her body and open water.
The sand gives nothing away.

She takes two steps and halts,
feels nothing. Today, she wants
to lose herself below her chest,
has never been in water so cold.

She wants to know if her heart
will finally stop skipping beats
and quiet or quit, this fist of muscle
from which she asks so much.

It's true that the more time you spend in a landscape, the more familiar it becomes. That spring, I learned when it wasn't okay to enter the water because the waves had an undertow I could feel against the soles of my feet in the shallows, and I watched for rip tides like the ones I saw as a child in California. Though I'd never lived by the sea, I was surprised by the respect with which I treated its dangers, but even more, by my growing familiarity and ease with it, which engendered a feeling of belonging to the place. It was an understanding I'd soon start to recognise in other parts of my life, too.

II.

My growing obsession with the sea didn't end with my plunges into cold water. At some point in the spring, I felt guilty that my writing had focused on a fictional character that bore no real relation to Dunbar. On the next few visits, I set out to write about its landmarks so that I could read poems that a Coastword audience might recognise.

I wanted to write about the Barns Ness Lighthouse (automated in 1986) and the idea of a lighthouse keeper lighting the light as his time and usefulness came to an end. I could imagine how he took his work of keeping others safe seriously, and how that work might have left him in perilous danger of losing himself when the machines finally replaced him. It was a terrific metaphor for motherhood: if I mothered well – with all the minutiae that that work entailed – I'd be out of a job at the end of my term. My children would travel on without me, having passed the overwhelming dangers of childhood, and then focusing (rightly) on their own new horizons.

The Last Keeper
— *the Barns Ness Lighthouse becomes automated in 1986*

When he lights this final lamp he knows
it will be extinguished, that no beacon can burn

across sea or land for a lifetime; even
daylight and darkness, no matter the season,

draw to a close. He polishes the silver and trims
the wick for old times' sake, wanting things

to be right and true, though no one else will know.
Then he keeps vigil, watching it burn through,

refuses food or water as if air is enough.
He knows what this means, his last night,

this last light; he knows from here on out,
  he is the only one in danger of darkness.

The cold sea water had started me wondering what I'd want for my own life when mothering ended. This wondering also coincided with a few instances of racism in my day-to-day life, as well as being regularly reminded that I wasn't *from* Scotland and that, as an outsider, I would never understand the unwritten rules for living here. People weren't sure where I was from, but even after twenty years in the UK, most people were clear that I'd never be British. I started wondering if I even *wanted* to grow old in this place that so often thought of me as a stranger, and what I could do to leave open other possibilities in my future. Are mothers stuck in the birthplaces of their children? Even if their children leave the country, do mothers need to stay and *be* the 'home' that grown children return to? Or could I choose this place for myself, even if it didn't want to choose me?

Storm Light
In the absolute dark of storm this light shines,
blinks, shines again as if morse-coded,

faster than the speed of sound, a howl
from a child, the wind against glass panes.

The guttering comes clean off the tacked felt roof.
Everything pinned down in daylight is upended.

In the absolute dark of storm hold the flash
of the lighthouse beacon between your hands.

Watch it flicker like a firefly, on and off,
burning and at rest, its back anchored

against the warmth of your lifeline,
just waiting for the right moment to fly.

III.

Around the same time as my Dunbar residency, a school-dad friend became ill with cancer. Olly is one of the kindest humans I've met in Scotland, gentle and thoughtful. He's also an extreme sportsman. His cancer was probably detected late *because* he was so healthy; his lung capacity was greater than that of ordinary mortals, so when he started showing signs of deterioration no one picked it up. When he announced he was ill, I engaged a little when I could with the family, dropping the odd meal and sending messages of support. But his illness struck me hard, shocked me like one of those cold-water dips – if *he* could get cancer, so could the rest of us.

Because of Olly's illness, I started mulling over the idea of attempting my long-held bucket list dream of running a marathon before I hit fifty, a couple of years away. But I didn't want to run just any marathon; I'd always wanted to run the New York City Marathon because my father had run it at the age of forty-seven, when I was still a teenager. I remembered him going out for long runs on Sundays with his running 'buddies' and remembered hearing about his finish. He ran with a friend who was injured, and even though the friend was running too slowly for them both, my father refused to leave the man's side for most of the race. Apparently, at mile sixteen, his friend insisted that he be left behind, and from there my father ran the final ten miles in under seven minutes a mile – a hugely impressive negative split, especially for someone his age. The photograph of him crossing the finish line at 3:33 – arms held high – still hangs in my parents' living room.

A few years after my father's race, I'd trained for a marathon myself. I put in long miles while at university, forgoing alcohol (a big deprivation at nineteen), eating and sleeping well for months, but I never made it to the race. In the end, I turned an ankle on the longest training run, having decided on one more lap of the campus to take me up to marathon length, to be sure I'd be able finish on the day. I didn't go to A&E or even ice the foot as I should have, and instead did what any foolish and disappointed young person would have done, which is to say I went out drinking and dancing all night. By morning, my foot was black from the top of the ankle to its sole, and for years after that, it hurt when I ran too long or too hard on it. I knew that running a marathon in my late forties would be a challenge because of that ankle, but also because (apart from cold-water immersion), I hadn't done any real exercise for years. Still, I signed up for the New York City Marathon – a chance to go home to New York for a visit, to push this newly-considered body of mine, and prove to myself that *I can do hard things* beyond cold-water swimming.

Early on, Olly came to the rescue. I saw his wife Jane – also a friend – on a train platform one morning and admitted that his cancer had inspired me to sign up for the marathon. I asked her whether it would be hard for him to hear about it, as he still wasn't exercising much yet, or whether she thought he'd be willing to help me prepare.

Please reach out. You're exactly the kind of project he needs right now, she said gently.

Olly found me a training plan, walked me through how I could approach the months of running and the day itself without doing too much scary research of my own. He acknowledged my reticence around having to have (or being able to afford) the 'latest' gear and lent me the few things I would absolutely need. We met every few weeks to check on my progress, and I saved up all my silly running questions for him rather than hitting google and the endless running forums. Early on in these meetings, when I said my legs were surprisingly sore, he suggested ice baths.

At our age – no offence, honest! – you're going to need some help to recover.

I explained that I did not, under any circumstances, have the willpower to lower my body into a bath of ice.

What about the sea, then? You've been talking about sea swimming this spring, so why don't you get in at the end of your runs and stretch off there?

That moment changed my relationship with cold water. Now, I wasn't getting in as a project, to write poems about another woman. I was getting in to help my body recover from the exertion of long runs in preparation for a marathon, one of my bucket-list dreams.

I told only a few close friends and my immediate family that I was training. But as the day approached, I let the broader world know I was going to run the race for the support that I knew would come. The advice friends gave me went largely unheeded – apart from starting out slow and speeding up if I felt okay. I hadn't done any of the recommended visualisations, or even looked up the route of the course – I'd left New York City to move to Britain in 1999 (and then Scotland in 2005) and wanted this marathon experience to feel like a surprise, while also feeling like coming home. A cousin sent her biggest take-home lesson from running a marathon:

Finishing is all in the mind. The 'marathon' is actually a mental exercise. If you believe you can do it, you can; the body has the capacity to endure so much more than running twenty-six miles.

Heeding the lesson from all those years ago, this time around I didn't run a full-length marathon beforehand to test out my capacity. I did what the training plan, Olly and my cousin told me to do: trusted that my body would get me across the line.

On the day itself, my oldest friend flew from Chicago to take care of me post-race, and another even hopped the line and ran a mile with me, telling me to slow down as I was burning around the course too fast. Other friends at home (including my self-appointed coach), cheered me along with messages that pinged in my out-of-reach pocket. I held back, not sure if I would hit the infamous 'wall', but when those around me started peeling off, being sick or needing to stop, I used my cold-water skill of checking in with my body to see how it was holding up. To my surprise, I felt good and so I sped up, making my last mile one of my fastest. I crossed the finish line with my arms held high, just like my father's arms in the picture I'd looked at a hundred times.

When I got back to Scotland, I didn't want to stop running, or getting into cold water. By then, I'd discovered the mountain reservoirs nearer to home in Edinburgh. I liked to disappear there for a few hours of running. I used those road-mile strengths to understand my strength, and quickly learned how far I could run before I'd need to stop. I took a tumble in January on a hill in icy conditions with absolutely nothing on me but a phone, but that didn't dampen my enthusiasm – instead, I realised how lucky I'd been. Bruised and sore, I messaged Olly when I got home to ask for a coffee to discuss what I *should* have been carrying with me that day, and he duly explained what I needed to carry in winter for emergencies.

Once I knew that I had what I needed on my body, I felt even more free. I could run for miles in the Pentlands without seeing anyone, and did so gladly, repeating my *I can do hard things* mantra when the going got tough. My old New York fear of coming across someone unsavoury, someone who could want to hurt me, dissipated: I figured they'd have to find me first, and I was fairly certain that I could outrun most people anyway. Ironically, it was the clear understanding of my own limits that gave me real strength and freedom. I'd hop into the nearest reservoir towards the end of a run and then put my clothes back on atop my wet pants and sports bra, knowing I didn't have far to go to get back to my car.

That spring, I was approaching the tipping point of having lived in Scotland longer than having lived anywhere else, and I wasn't sure if I'd choose to go 'home' to the USA, if given the chance. On those long runs, I gave myself permission to ask what *I* really wanted without reference to others, and allowed myself to sit with the experience of not knowing the answer. What I did know was that I was strong enough, in body and spirit, to be able to live through the answer, whenever it came.

As it turns out, it didn't take long, arriving one morning in February on a long circuit through the Pentlands. Off in a world of my own, I suddenly heard a voice in my head say *I am home – the out-of-doors is home*. It was such a strong sensation that I stopped mid-run, mid-path beside a reservoir. *THIS is home,* I said aloud, nodding along with my own thought, *right here*. On reflection, that sense of belonging came from the knowledge of my own body's strength (*I CAN do hard things*), along with a familiarity with a place I felt was becoming not only recognisable but familiar. What is belonging, if not familiarity with the world around you, and understanding you have a place, a space within it?

Up there in the hills, miles from the nearest road, I felt more at home than I'd ever felt in Edinburgh. A heron was watching me from the water, it hadn't flown off when I'd stopped. Nothing questioned my right to run that path: the trees didn't ask where I was from, how long I'd been there, or whether I'd stay. I felt like myself in those woods, and in the reservoir where I would go on to dip and stretch at the end of my run, judging the cold, paying attention for the signs that it was time to get out. I knew – I really *understood* – what my body was capable of, and exactly how far it could take me. *I know these hills and valleys. I can keep myself safe here*, I thought, *which means I am safe here. Maybe this means I'm home.*

GRANDMA APPLES

Alice Tarbuck

I'm weary with my former toil,
Here I will sit and rest awhile:
Under the shadow I will be
Of Jesus Christ the apple tree.

Rev. Richard Hutchins, 1761

It is early spring now and we are taking my Grandmother home, home to the high point on the moors where she was born, in a stone house built on a steep slope. This time, we don't have to worry about finding suitable accommodation for her: a hotel without too many stairs, where the chef will agree to cooking a single, plain poached egg for her supper. This time she sits beside me in a slim purple tube of surprising weight, taking up barely any space at all.

I have no idea if she will be glad to be home.

She will come to rest in the place she spoke of most often. Had she been given a choice, I am not sure she would ever have left. That has to be good enough.

The car is full of silence. Each of us, I know, is thinking of her. Her presence is amplified far beyond her living form. She is a comfortable haunting, one we all share, that we won't speak about. This journey might be fairly straightforward – five hours, winding down through Scotland, weaving among the dense borderlands and then into Cumbria, the landscape no less undulating, dog-legging to Yorkshire – but it encompasses every aspect of her life. We drive across the country as if we are leafing through a photograph album, each absorbed in our personal highlights. We travel through the land and through our memories, on this quest to lay our matriarch to rest. We find her in the Tebay services, looking out at the ducks on their pond. We find her in the 'Welcome to England' sign in which she had always delighted. We find her in the steepening slopes and the wildering moors, as they sing with their history. Grandma is with us – and in this final journey, all her journeys are brought together.

I can tell you all the places my Grandmother ever journeyed: there aren't many. She was born in Upper Mill, in the West Riding of Yorkshire. She moved to Manchester, the only child taken when her mother remarried. When she herself married, she moved again – ending up in Ongar, Essex, a suburb of cul-de-sacs and domestic expectations. Her husband, a keen diver, sometimes took her on holiday to Spain – with his diving club, and both of their children. There is no sense whatsoever that she enjoyed it, keeping control of two boys in the aching heat of a foreign hotel whilst her husband spent all day submerged in a cool, blue world she never shared. My grandmother came to Scotland when I was born, leaving the sense and clemency of England behind for a frontier that might as well have been rural Russia. She didn't trust the populace and she didn't like the weather. But then, my grandma disliked going anywhere. What she wanted most was for the world to stand still and wait for her to arrange it into perfect order, the very opposite of travel.

What is her place, then, in a collection of women travellers? When she travelled it was against her will, with bodily and psychological difficulty. The way I travel now can look a little bit like hers – but this is not because I dislike the change of scene, the excitement. My travel is restricted by my chronic illness, which makes the unknown perilous: where will pain come, how will it be managed, how will I balance my desire to absorb the world fully with my body's need to rest, rest, rest? Two women less suited to travel-stories you could not imagine, and so this tale is about the way that extraordinary journeys can affect and change our lives even when we don't undertake them. It is a story about evolution. A story about the power of apples, and a quest for a resting place.

My Grandmother had a beautiful garden. It was the truest possible manifestation of her desire for stillness – a place where things would take root over time, that would need continual effort. You cannot simply leave a garden to go off gallivanting – there are always things to be done. Grandma tended to her garden the way that was fashionable in her generation: black earth between clumps of plants, the borders of her lawn regimented. I am sure she would have told you that the greatest glory of her garden were her sweet peas, waving from the trellis. But for her granddaughters, there was one unquestionable treasure in that garden – her apple tree.

The apple tree was squat, a short trunk supporting branches which, despite pruning, always resembled a ball of tangled roots. The apples which it produced were special for their profusion, their extraordinary scent and their deliciousness. They were 'Discovery' apples – a name redolent with exotic promise. Discovery apples were, indeed, 'discovered' in the 1940s when an Essex farmer grew open-pollinated apple seedlings from the variety Worcester Pearmain. These young trees came to the attention of Jack Matthews, a nurseryman from Sussex, who brought the Discovery variety to the commercial apple market in 1962. Discovery trees require regular pruning, so vigorous is their outlay – but they are poor 'keepers' and the fruit doesn't store. If not eaten when fresh, their skin wrinkles unattractively and they take on a mealy quality. Common wisdom understands them as poor 'cookers', too, although I do not agree. They make a marvellous, delicately flavoured stewed apple, if one is prepared to sacrifice firm textured pieces. As a child, I thought they were the most delicious apple in the world.

They are also beautiful. Ripe, the apples are scarlet, and this bleeds through the skin and into the first layer of their flesh. They take on the allure of the mythic apple – perhaps this red corona indicates poison; perhaps the leak of forbidden knowledge into the fruit; perhaps, the blood of Christ himself. Finding the little thumbnail of red under the skin was considered a great treat, making the apple even more delectable. Apple season meant fresh apples, stewed apple, and apple pies made with homemade, wholemeal pastry. Grandma would walk them over to our house, still hot, carefully wrapped in a tea towel, to be eaten after supper. Plastic shopping bags of apples would be delivered until the fruit bowl was overflowing, and my sister and I – champion apple eaters though we were – could barely keep up. Any excess of this bounty Grandma would carefully wash, dry, and leave on her front garden wall for passers-by.

It was extraordinary, that such a little tree could produce so much fruit.

As I grew older, I could stew the apples myself. They formed part of the rhythm of university – a race against the end of the long summer holiday, to see if any apples would be ripe before I had to leave. Then, when I moved back to Edinburgh, the apple harvest became something I could do with Grandma, talk to her about. I would lug overflowing bags back to shared flats, make crumble upon crumble – unlike her, I've never mastered pastry. My Grandma's apples became something that my friends looked forward to. Most of them never met her, but so many of them ate her apples, gathered around my table every autumn. I like to think of all the places that her apples have travelled – slipped into pockets and rucksacks, taken home as leftovers to houses all over Scotland. A network of apples, extending from one still point. Two of my dearest friends came to her funeral, and I thought of all the times they had enjoyed what she had grown, how fondly they remembered her through this generosity. Although my grandmother grew frailer, the apples demanded the same of her, year on year. Her pruning of the tree became cursory, then ceased altogether, but she never stopped picking them, cleaning them up, popping them on her garden wall for folks to take.

Until, of course, she did. But we are not yet there on our journey. We are still by the apple tree, as the day around us slips into evening.

We might think of the apple, much like my Grandmother, as being quintessentially of the British Isles. We take great pride in our apples. After the Black Death had ravaged the populace and the cultivation of apples had ceased to be a priority, Henry VIIII himself instructed his fruiterer to cultivate new varieties, and plant them in his orchard in Kent. We have apples named after Shakespeare characters (the Kentish 'Falstaff' of the 1980s), and a proud culture of cider-production in the South-West of England. Apples, and their role in our cuisine and culture, feel inextricably linked with British identity. However, for all that apples are part of our cultural heritage, a little exploration reveals that – like much else claimed as 'British' – they originate elsewhere. This is a truth my Grandmother struggled with: her love of country was embedded in both the ideological and the material, leading to her preference for British wool, British food, a British version of world history. Yet despite her aversion to travel even she could admit that the apple, like so many now-native fruits and vegetables, had more exotic origins.

The apple is extraordinary in its existence, proliferation, and evolution. The ephemeral and the eternal – deep time, and the shallow breadth of human life – all tangled up together in something you can hold in one hand. The apple tree seems to exist on a very human scale and feels, even when encountered in the wild, somehow domestic. My grandmother was ninety-six when she died. The average age for an apple tree is around thirty-five years – she could have seen two apple trees from pip to death, and still had almost the lifespan of a third left over. There is something troubling about this – perhaps the childish assumption that humans, so small, so unsteadily bipedal, ought to die long before trees, so rooted and part of the earth.

But although trees are rooted, their history is one of journeys, spanning the grove and the globe. Whilst each individual tree might stand still, their fruits and seeds disperse across the globe. Trees are travellers, and ancient ones – perhaps Tolkien's Ents, the giant tree-walkers, were a more accurate depiction of trees than we might at first imagine. Certainly, apple trees have a history far longer than the life of my Grandmother – far longer than the span of the human race. The apple originated in the Tien Shan mountains of Kazakhstan and predates human evolution, with the 'earliest fossil records of the family appearing in the mid-Cretaceous period, about 85 to 100 million years ago'.[14] They flourished there in their undomesticated form, sour and small and wild. Apples trees have survived an ice age, and their hard-coated seeds were initially transported across the globe by megafauna. Much, much later, humans spread apples along the Silk Road. The paths that we make across the world are littered with what we treasure – and fruit is a waymarker, an indication

14   Gayle Brandow Samuels, 'Apples: Core Issues', *Enduring Roots: Encounters with Trees, History, and the American Landscape*, Rutgers University Press, 1999.

of human presence, a beacon of living archaeology.

Apples have significance in Christian imagery – the apple tree was often considered a parallel to the body of Christ, given in sacrifice for the good of mankind. This may be due to the reference to the Biblical tree of life, or the apple tree in the Song of Solomon which is understood to be a metaphor for Jesus. My Grandmother, a life-long Christian, would have enjoyed these representations of faith adorning her home, even if she never made the connection. Additionally, apples can be successfully stored, either dried or packed in straw, and have a significant role in cultural consciousness because of this. By growing apples, my grandmother was continuing traditions which have been around for hundreds of years, if not longer. But they are not simply helpful, beautiful plants; apples have a trickster quality – they produce endless variety.

The apple has such enormous heterozygosity that the same variety cannot reliably be bred from pips. Instead, grafting is employed – the attachment of varietal branches on to standard rootstocks. If you plant the pips, you're likely to get a plant which is wildly different from its parents. The dependable passing on of similar characteristics is joyfully disrupted in favour of novelty, making orchard management a very different game from the management of other crops. One such example of this extraordinary heterozygosity is the old Scottish apple varietal, the 'Bloody Ploughman', with its blood-red hue and curious ribbed shape. This ancient variety had seen a sharp wane in its popularity, but is springing up once more in orchards, most notably in the Millennium Garden of Floors Castle in the Scottish Borders. The Bloody Ploughman carries, as one might expect, quite the origin story. It seems to me a particularly Scottish piece of mythology – the sweet apple wrapped in layers of deceit and murder. It is alleged that a gamekeeper shot dead a ploughman who had been caught stealing apples from the Megginch Estate in Perthshire. When the poor ploughman's body was returned to his wife, she found the stolen apples in his pockets. Heartbroken, she threw them onto a rubbish heap. One of the resulting seedlings bore apples of a deep, blood red. These pips, carelessly tossed, did not grow into the same variety as the tree from which they had come. Instead, they developed into an entirely new apple variety, named after its unfortunate originator.[15]

We are not subject to the same heterozygosity. As humans, we know that the apple often does not fall far from the tree. When I was young, I felt different from my Grandmother, with her moral absolutism and attention to order. As she aged, and then became ill, my understanding of our similarities grew. It wasn't just the apples – although they were symptomatic of our shared love of fruit, of the processes of growing and preserving. My Grandmother's dementia brought out first her fury, but then her sweetness. She smiled easily, small things began to delight her. Historically night-marish to buy presents for, she became transfixed by the joys of Christmas, delightedly unwrapping her gifts and treasuring them. Always conscious of her figure, she transformed into someone happy to eat cake without castigating herself. Whilst her remaining time here dwindled, she became briefly more attuned to earthly joys. She reminded me of myself as a child, embodied and delighted. She wanted to sing songs and listen to stories. She held our hands in hers. As she began her journey away from us forever, she grew closer to us, for a time.

It was during this time that my obsession started. I had known for a while that eventually, there would come a day when I would have eaten the final apple from that little Discovery tree, would

15 'Bloody Ploughman Apple'. *Scottish Food Guide*. Archived from the original on 1 December 2018. Retrieved 30 November 2018.

have smelled the skin for the final time, would never again chew down to the core in delight. I dreaded it, some proxy for her loss which I could not yet comprehend in its fullness. The apples gained a new importance. Whenever I went round, I would go and stand by the tree, looking up through the branches, questing for signs of ripeness, of growth. But it is impossible to stave off time and its ravages. Impossible to join someone on that final journey. When they are gone, we have our memories, and whatever it is they have left behind. I could not keep the apple tree. I could not keep hold of the apples. Something began in me then, which grew and grew over the next two years. Apple-creep, bringing their presence in my brain from a background hum to a knife-sharp fixation. Apples were my quest object, the holy grail of connection to my Grandmother, and I was the gallant knight who would journey to seek its treasure. I took up my sword, and the five-minute walk from our house to hers became as perilous a quest as that which Galahad undertook. What would I find at the end of it, and was I prepared?

Although it was a particular fixation, my delight in gathering fruit did not originate with Grandma's apples, you understand. I'd always been a keen forager, scouring railway paths for brambles, and partial to the odd windfall. In those years of her decline my interest burst its banks. Now, I couldn't bear the thought of a single apple going to waste, anywhere. Some impulse in me needed to gather them all, stew them, preserve them. The quest gained urgency, gained a symbolic importance, its perimeters widened, and I could not help but ride out.

You cannot stave off bad news, but you can build up store cupboards to get through it. Fiercely, madly, erratically, I ransacked autumn for all of her spoils. I dreamed of apples, of her tree bowed under the weight of its harvest. I dreamed of peeling them with a paring knife, bare feet on my parents' kitchen tiles, the peel coming off in one long spiral. I saw them behind closed eyes, bobbing in cold water, softening under sugar. Dream-apples, transforming into something I could hold. It is not a shock that apples play a significant part in myths and folk-practices from around the world – it was apples that the Gods of Asgard ate to keep their youth; it was a golden apple which Paris had to present to the most beautiful Goddess of all. For me, they were an attempt at magic, to pull the ordinary world toward me, wring from it every last drop of sweetness, to delay, or soften, or bargain away the outcome which I could not stop.

It's funny to think about, a woman in her late thirties at a stately home in the Borders, trying to shove her pockets full of heirloom windfalls in a scrawny orchard, in full sight of the windows. They had all sorts – cookers, eaters, strange ribbed ones which must have been ancient. The wasps were drunk on all of the broken apples over the ground, a low hum in the grass. Everything felt unnaturally still, as if the air was too thick to breathe. And every breath was heavy with apple-scent. My in-laws were visiting; I should have been working on my good impression. Instead, I was feral, scrabbling in the long grass, determined that not a decent apple would be left after my ministrations. My partner had to drag me away, more or less, when I was already weighed down and near hysterical.

It wasn't just there, either. Up on the hillside behind the house, beating the grass under the single apple tree, a wanderer from the farmland below. Bags and bags of other people's overflow – 'oh, you've got too many to deal with? I'd love some!'. Crab apples from the ornamental tree on my dog-walking route, the fruit no larger than a cherry. Hundreds of apples. Every single one washed and sorted, stewed and frozen, or slipped into vodka. The earth couldn't give me what I wanted – a world without death, without my Grandmother falling apart and unstitching the matriarchal hold she'd had over us all for decades – so I took what it could give. Whatever fruit it grew, I was going to hoard it. The quest, hopeless and against death, took me across the landscape – I explored hidden corners, begged favours of friends, tales of their trees from their lands, journeyed through stories as I tried to find meaning on my journey of loss.

Amid my feverish foraging, my Grandmother became very unwell. She spent a spell in hospital and was then moved into a nursing home. These journeys were strange for her – it was simply that her legs gave out one day, and the ambulance men found her perfectly calm, stuck in her chair. The journey from home to hospital was made on a stretcher; the journey into the nursing home was, for her, gentle, in the kind hands of nurses and orderlies. She took nothing with her, asked for nothing to be brought, although we brought her so many things. For me, that was a summer of frenetic movement, running between the fast pace of my job and the treacled air of the ward. We would sit together and talk. Well. I would talk. Mostly she listened, eyes closed, or almost. The conversation she could make made little sense, adrift from context, place and time. She was journeying, travelling between this plane and the next. She hadn't wanted to leave her house, but once she was in hospital she didn't ask after it, or the garden. Instead, she seemed to exist both in the present moment and in the deep past, somewhere none of us could follow. All the years she had read me stories I attempted to return to her – reading poems, singing hymns. All of her favourites, the ones she had grown up with, and taught to me. She enjoyed them, I think. The nurses were so kind to her, but she began to lose her ability to swallow, and wouldn't take food or liquid. She was preparing to leave, her final journey letting her free of all of her earthly suffering, taking her to rest in the place she believed she would go to, that summer-land, that eternal orchard of bliss.

In the dog days of August, her apples ripened. Every day we had gone in to check on her house, we had inspected them, urging them on. We knew then that this would be our last harvest, thought, perhaps, that if only she could see them, they could pour some of their extraordinary resilience into her. Perhaps we even thought they would shake her from her reverie, let her impart some words of wisdom and love before she left. What happened instead is that we picked them and cleaned them, my mother and I. We brought bags of them to the nurses, explained how proud she had been of the apples, how much she would have wanted them to taste what she had grown. Some apples we stewed for her, hoping that they might tempt her to eat. We kept back the nicest one – the most extraordinary apple, perfectly round, and deep scarlet, exquisitely perfumed – washed it carefully, and took it to her.

I wish I could say that the apple affected some miracle – that it undertook the magical work I so badly wanted it to. It didn't, of course. It undertook a much more subtle magic. A far more necessary one. My mother placed the apple carefully in my Grandmother's hands, as she lay propped up in bed. Explained that it was hers, that she had grown it. We told her that, as always, there was a bowl of them on the wall for the neighbours to help themselves. She held the apple gently, as one might hold a fragile globe, or a baby's head. She didn't say anything at all, but she did smile. Perhaps it did not matter to her at all, that final harvest. I rather suspect that we had undertaken the rigmarole of it selfishly – not for her, but for ourselves, to create some sort of memorial, some sort of goodbye. The living wait upon the dying, but they also wait upon themselves, bringing themselves succour through acts of kindness, acts of small magic. The apple sat by her bedside as she faded into memory. It was still perfectly ripe, perfuming the air of her room when she finally passed. I had, like a medieval knight, found the perfect object, revered it, and brought it to one I loved. And, as in almost all such quests and journeys, the prize was not in the final moment, but rather in what I had learned about her, and myself, in the process.

She is not long gone, and yet it seems aeons. She is resting, now, with a long view over the hills of the West Riding of Yorkshire, watching the weather move across the ancient stone. Her apples are still in my freezer – so, too, are pots of those fever-apples, the desperate refusal to let anything go. I am saving them all for special occasions – small domestic things – feeding my stepchildren, having friends round. When we eat them, we talk about her. We thank her for what she grew, and what she gave. I do not believe that the dead are ever far from us, even on their journeys into the next world. I can conjure her in the smell of Imperial Leather soap. She can be found in the garden shed, by the neat bundle of canes in the corner. In sweet peas and stewed apples. There are spells for bringing everybody back, out of the darkness of ash and memory, but I use hers sparingly. I believe she has earned her rest.

I presume she has found heaven as neat as a cricket-lawn, brimming with good soil and drawers of pressed handkerchiefs scented with linen water. I hope that there are orchards where she can walk, good greengrocers with tiled floors and modest prices. I hope she has a good paring knife, and no pain when she rolls the pastry out. I hope she puts out apples, if she wishes to, for neighbours who stop and talk to her. I find her in every apple tree, and I love her there, the sure branches and the sweet fruit opening like a window onto the next world, where I can glimpse her. The apple trees that she outlived will, I hope, continue far after we are all of us gone, their seeds carried into the future by goodness knows what, perhaps some strange animal I cannot yet imagine, perhaps the children of my friends and family, who carry her memory, the taste of those apples, beyond the furthest horizons of our knowing.

FROM OUR OWN CORRESPONDENT

Jemma Neville

What do Margaret Thatcher, Julia Roberts and Beyoncé all have in common?

(This sounds like a trivia question in a board game you would have made us play. Blue wedge of the pie, people and places, 2020s edition.)

Twins! All these women gave birth to boy-girl twins. And twins, I have discovered, is the response to many questions I have as a mother, navigating the journey of parenting multiples. Prime Ministers, actors and singers may have some extra help at home. For the rest of us, we must follow the markers left by those that travelled ahead – no matter the path taken or how many babies carried – because women are always carrying more than first appears.

Above our kitchen sink hangs a watercolour of Salisbury Crags. The pleasing sweep of Edinburgh's old town skyline expands below muted hues of green parkland. You painted this familiar landscape many years ago and assigned it to me in the careful allocation of who was to get what among the materiality and nostalgia that clings to a life.

The surrounding pine frame is out of fashion with contemporary tastes and the mount is spotted in places from condensation and soap suds. Still, I look closely at this painting several times a day because, like all the women before me, I am often stood at the kitchen sink, cleaning dishes and wiping tiny hands. To be careful – full of care – requires close-looking. And if you've got to be doing these things, whether as a 1960s housewife or a 2020s not-a-wife, it's nice to have a view to look upon.

You dismissed it as not one of your better paintings, saying that the perspective and scale are all wrong. The spire of St Giles Cathedral is taller on the horizon than the Castle ramparts further up the Royal Mile and the geometric lines of the Forth Rail Bridge appear too prominent. But isn't perspective about where you are standing? And from where I am stood – not quite old and not quite young, with three babies, a partner, parents, many jobs, rural living and all the mental load that passes for love and responsibility – there is grandeur in this view of midlife.

We used to walk together on Salisbury Crags. We scrambled along the Radical Road scree and sat among the flowering gorse that is timeless and so forever smells of coconut shampoo. As my steps widened and yours turned toward home, I talked about solo travels living and working abroad – from UN tribunals in Sierra Leone, to backpacking in Costa Rica, yoga ashrams in India and helicopter flights across Greenland. The pages of my Rough Guides and Lonely Planets were bookmarked with tickets, the margins scrawled with phone numbers – at a time when accumulating airmiles was not regarded as obscenely privileged. You encouraged all these adventures and homecomings, extolling to your young granddaughters about the pitfalls of being *stuck at home with a bucketful of nappies.*

Now, the journeys I make are plodding at a toddler's pace around a sodden field, with talk of puddles and blackbirds in place of politics or literature. We live on a stretch of The John Muir Way and our daily plods are surely *the dirt paths of life* that the lone explorer and famous conservationist had in mind, were he to have been a woman carrying small children, together with their balance bikes, helmets, teddies and enough snacks to wild camp in the Sierra Nevada.

I carry my three increasingly heavy children – twins and their elder brother whom we grieve – bundled onto my front and back like an expedition sherpa wearing Babybjörn and lipstick. If you were still here, Gran, I know that you would appreciate a nod to glamour in muddy times. If I douse myself in a cloud of Elnett hairspray, I can be instantly transported back to your peach-coloured bathroom suite, with its mirrored cupboards full of scents and sprays.

All of us women are adept in the art of holding things. When the twins were new-born, I perfected a kitten-hold technique to be able to scoop up one baby from his bouncer chair with a clutch of romper fabric in my left hand, while still nursing his sister in the hold of my right. I learnt this hold from one of your other granddaughters, also a mother of twins. And as mine have grown into small children needing to safely enter or exit my car parked on a busy road, I must grip one twin's hand while barrelling the other into a rugby ball hold. Perhaps an octopus is the better creature metaphor, with their eight, resilient limbs and three beating hearts hidden beneath the waves?

Animal instincts have taught me that twins multiply love many times over but can also divide attention and energy with the thousands of micro-conflicts and choices that accumulate throughout a day from first waking. *My TURN! Pick me! Mama, ME next, me!* These howls of fury from cots might funnel through me like a relentless headwind but they are the loud cries I longed to hear from my first born, a premature baby. Every day – and some days more than others – bereavement is an additional, needy child that requires constant feeding, lifting, and settling. All three babies were born within a year. Irish triples, some call it.

On daily expeditions in the countryside, we might hear the *choo choo* of the fast train to London. The twins and I wave vigorously from the edge of the track to passengers on their way to meetings and dates and experiences in the big city. If someone waves back, it is both thrilling and exposing. Our days are full of noticing and emptied of plans.

I notice that my body is a map. There are steep, shaded contours in the centre to mark peaks and plateaus from pregnancies and stretch marks. Favourite routes are highlighted as smile-lines around the corners of my eyes and mouth. Lay me open and the tears from childbirth and death let light and dark pour in. I fold all this up into the concertina of a woman's frame and tuck it into the neat spaces and distances afforded.

I notice too that my bed has become a basecamp. The aching tiredness of broken sleep from attending to others' needs combines with an insomnia from anxiety that creeps into my bed like an uninvited, jealous lover. There are warm elbows and knees under and over the covers as I toss and turn and cartoon theme tunes loop in my head. In the morning, I awake to find that the chubby bedfellows have eaten all my mental energy and drunk me dry of creative imagination. And yet, in the inarticulate and fragmented words that do show up, I know there is something urgent to say about the common monotony of raising children as best as possible. I want to say that it is heroic and joyful, exploratory, and dangerous.

I therefore keep a log or diary of fieldnotes to record the travel conditions. It doesn't matter that my handwriting is near-illegible and the content quite mundane – because this is a diary to be written, not read, and when I'm gone only its subjects, my children, will care to decipher its full code.

The sporadic entries are sparse, matter of fact accounts of family life that document developmental milestones – a first tooth, crawl or weaning – alongside the banality of weather and news headlines. It is a first-person account of the isolation that coexists with laughter and intimacies when traversing the foothills of motherhood. Here, if you like, is my own Lonely Planet guidebook.

However, I am not alone in time-travel correspondence. Grandma Isobel, you also kept parenting diaries. You told us where to find them – in the drawer of an old bureau – warning about the stifling boredom you once feared from *making sponge puddings and painting nails all day* while living as a suburban housewife. I didn't consider until recently that the diaries could be read like a travel log and now, decades later, I can attempt to translate some of their foreign correspondence. Perhaps life only makes sense read backwards.

Your diaries, entitled with self-deprecating irony *A Trivial Life*, converse with well-known titles from the same era by Betty Freidan, Simone de Beauvoir and Doris Lessing, as they sit side by side on my bookshelves. This is how they begin:

Isobel, October 1958
Both in bath at bedtime and quite hilarious. Youngest son not keen to drink much but he is the healthiest, happiest child. Occasional catarrh. Crawls on his tummy all over the floor and sits pulling toys out of his box. Five more teeth through – no bother. Takes soup and cereal. So active! Two scratches from Susie.

I translate that you were discovering as much about yourself as a new mother as about your new-born infant and that, contrary to your warnings to granddaughters about the hard work of babies, you were happy.

Susie was a cat! From the future looking back, I know that the scratching feline became more of a risk to your son's asthma, then undiagnosed. You later stopped keeping cats and, more importantly, stopped smoking. This lengthened your life considerably. Your own (single) mother, Stella, died of lung cancer within a decade of the diary entry, and it devasted you. The baby boy became a doctor specialising in respiratory medicine.

And, in the 1950s, health visitors advised weaning babies as early as a few weeks' old. Longer-term breastfeeding was frowned upon. The NHS was in its infancy. You wouldn't have experienced things like ultrasound scans.

Whereas Doris Lessing had her *Golden Notebook*, yours are in a red school jotter and are a mix of baby milestones from the 1950s and a ritual documenting of *a week in the life*, spanning 1965–2015.

28 October 1965

The busy spell should be ending soon. Age thirty-seven, sons nine and seven … Early start and I set off to school too. Dreadful weather. Collected new evening dress and later attended painting class. Letter of appointment arrived with wrong salary scale … Darling youngest son went on bike in a downpour of rain and bought me a birthday present – powder, lipstick and three puffs.

This tells me that returning to work part-time was liberating and that the family had become newly middle-class after knowing abject poverty a generation before. Unlike myself, you didn't have childcare support. But you also weren't expected to both work and parent full-time. 1965 is two years before the moon landing. It must have seemed like anything was possible.

I know you were tired – many of the diary entries conclude by saying so – but what else were you holding onto or carrying with difficulty? Were you frustrated that your education and career was fragmented? Were you aware of the absence of paternity leave or grandparent support? Did you wish for a daughter? Then, as now, it seems anything but not everything was possible. And has any mother of young children ever reported feeling relaxed and rested?

My own logs, from 2020 onward, are held in the brown parcel paper of a ledger or worn sketchbook, as befits grubby and guilt-soaked opportunities snatched for writing. There are some photographs and pressed leaves in the back pages, together with a list of first words. Two or three years into my motherhood journey, I can look back and read into what I was trying to communicate or warn about in the brief words and ellipses. The pause between entries might also say something. Here are some samples, in italics, in which identifying names or overtly personal details have been removed by referring to my children as T1, T2 and B1. Any interpretation notes are underneath.

Jemma, 21 October 2021

Aster, guelder rose and frogs in the garden. Huge spiders in bathroom. Skein of geese overhead. Age thirty-nine. T1 and T2 are six weeks old. B1 born one year ago. My mum singing to babies, T2 watching football on TV with his daddy. Daily pram push around field. Wet. Meteor shower at night (tail of Halley's Comet apparently). Full moon.

Humanitarian crisis in Afghanistan, preparations for COP26 climate conference in Glasgow, soaring energy prices.

What I meant to say is that seasonal changes matter because they punctuate the passing of time and prove that the babies are getting bigger and stronger. I also yearned to focus solely on one baby wholly.

Having the help of my own mother felt like I was anchored to something solid and true. Parenting has given me new respect for everything my own mother did, and does, for me.

It was six weeks since I had travelled further than the perimeter of the cottage garden. I was afraid of the wider world of violence.

I loved the domestic hum of sport on TV and my partner dreaming of all the games they will watch and play together.

26 November 2021

Cairngorms holiday! Our first getaway. Long drive broken up with a feeding stop in Tesco carpark. Twins met my parents' dog for the first time. Big smiles. Watched a lot of telly. Forest walks at Loch an Eilein, Invertromie meadow and Glen Feshie. Learnt that lichen on the birch tree's called Old Man's beard. First snow arrived, Storm Arwen. Fish biryani. So good to have a change of scene and slightly less laundry.

I think this diary entry is trying to communicate a sense of achievement, in referencing feeding and a return to proper cooking. However, in hindsight, the thing I most remember about the trip was getting lost on the (circular) walk around Loch an Eilein and having to tandem breastfeed on the forest floor. This felt slightly irresponsible, primal, and satisfying all at once. We argued about the navigation, the timekeeping and who forgot to bring mittens for the babies.

Also, no one warned me about how much laundry would come to dominate my one precious life. And about all the STUFF, or expedition kit. Packing, carrying, assembling, arranging, buying, selling, unpacking stuff. Could it be that clothes washing and sorting is an attempt to assert control and order during chaos?

22 February 2022

Much more head and neck control, soon be sitting I suppose. T1 rolling! A friend visited ahead of travels to South Africa. Took some beautiful photos. New baby bath purchased – shaped like a dolphin. A shame that no one else getting very clean or warm with our ongoing water pressure and boiler problems. Porridge and strawberries in highchair.

Russia invades Ukraine. Date for lifting all remaining Covid restrictions announced.

Six hours solid sleep at night! Fluke?!

25 February 2022

Yes, a fluke.

I want to tell my past self that sleep got much, much better. And that I fixed our water problems with assertive emailing. Conflict resolution, negotiation, budgeting, time management, and advocacy are transferable skills from family to life admin (and travelling).

Lots of people visited and photographed the new-born babies, but many months subsequently passed when no friends visited me home alone with two toddlers. When I needed a moment to myself, I used to hide in the bathroom, scrolling through photos on my phone of people I used to know living their lives outside of the home.

16 March 2022

Poor twins teething. Missing B1 and wondering how he would look at this age. Donated old snowsuits to Ukraine Community Appeal. Picked daffodils. Braved the twin sling at the beach. F'ing laundry. Calpol. Grandpa babysitting. Went to Nitin Sawney concert in town. Relieved to have seated tickets.

Nazanin Zaghari-Ratcliffe released from Iranian prison. Census data recorded.

The twin sling walk is still memorable to me. A stranger strode across the beach to pat me enthusiastically on the back – as though I was a very good spaniel – exclaiming "Well done, clever girl!" on seeing that the twins were a boy and a girl. This charted among other twin bingo exchanges, such as "Are they identical?", and personal dislikes of mine: "Oh, double trouble!" and "The baby factory is closed!".

30 March 2022
Jemma had a maternity keeping in touch today in the office. Late home because trains cancelled to accommodate the Queen travelling from Edinburgh Waverley to Balmoral. Twins at their dad's café. Eating omelette strips, toast and mango.

It is weird how regularly I refer to myself in the third person when parenting. And that I verbalised internal thoughts to get external validation from non-verbal babies: *"Ah, we've made it home in one piece, you've definitely earned a big coffee, Mama!"*

I interpret that the many references to trains in my diary is because it is impossible to singlehandedly lift a double buggy and two children over a railway bridge to safely reach the platform, or to cross four lanes of dual carriageway to get to a bus stop. This is something I never thought about before. I notice, too, that rocking a pram is now in my muscle memory and I still sway back and forth when pushing a shopping trolley, alone, around the supermarket.

Food features in many of the entries because being able to feed your children good, nutritious food is one of life's pleasures and privileges, as is watching a two-year-old eat an ice cream.

25 October 2022

A new Prime Minister, Rishi Sunak, and the UK's first as British Asian (still a Tory). T1 and T2 full of the cold – a day of worrying about the causes of recurrent chest problems. Testing negative for Covid. Twins can now climb onto furniture. Evening – improvised crashmats with yoga props – tested by hurling myself off the back of the sofa. Onto series five of This is Us series.

29 October 2023

In Glasgow, visiting in-laws. Looking at old family photographs from Pakistan in the 1940s and '50s. Dal and paratha. At home, boiler on the brink, again. Writing deadline. Tulips planted.

Worsening humanitarian situation in Gaza. Many angry protests. How to explain to small children? UK Covid Inquiry shown WhatsApp message exchange, revealing total disregard to peoples' safety.

1 December 2023

Snow and ice. Helping in café. Had coffee break with my uncle who has discovered Gran's diaries. In the evening, dragged my own family to village Christmas lights switch-on. We were late, as always, so missed the lights and carols. Twins high on orange squash and shortbread. Both ran onto the stage, crashing loudly through the winter wonderland scene. Got asked politely to remove children. Northern lights seen by many, but not by us.

I translate that I was nostalgic – in the sense of a yearning – for old networks and community. As the twins' voices have increased in volume and confidence, mine has wavered. It is as though I have lost all recognition of the person I once was. Though I suspect that all mothers go through this metamorphosis – the becoming of another.

Grandma, I wish that you had known me at this time in life and we could have spoken about these things and more. However, through reading and translating your notes, we are time-travellers together – chatting across the arc of a century. One day in the future, I will bundle up the collected record and leave them to the next generation to make sense of.

Twins are known to be experts in translation. Cryptophasia is the term for the secret speech between twins, both identical and fraternal. Language therapists report that over half of young twins develop their own twin vernacular which they use to communicate only with each other, and which is completely unintelligible to speakers of the parents' languages. It is possible that this phenomenon is caused by the greater care-giving demands made on parents of twins and thus less time outside the home and more intensive interaction between siblings (something else for mothers to feel guilty about).

My son and daughter – your great-grandchildren – are no exception. They have developed their own onomatopoeic vocabulary including names for one another that are different from the names we gave them. As when negotiating space and nutrients within the womb, the twins' relationship is symbiotic. If one falls over, the other dives to the ground in a performative show of sympathy and, also, a plea for attention.

My way of coping with the greater care-giving demands when the babies were small was to drill down on routine. Getting the babies to sleep in sync was paramount to the whole family's wellbeing. And so, in the beginning, their father and I kept sentry duty at night of shifts alternating between bed and sofa. We found that four hours was the minimum level of rest required to safely function. Like this, and contrary to all the Danish parenting manuals, very little was baby-led.

The briefest of handover intelligence about feeding, winding, and changing was exchanged as we swapped essential supplies of expressing bottles, cake and tv remote. Oxytocin and caffeine flooded our veins. If one or other of us managed breakfast *and* a shower, feelings of resentment, empathy and affection combined. Maternity leave came and went in a fog and if I hadn't jotted occasional postcards, I would have forgotten its many precious moments of handholding and song.

As a writer, putting words on a page is my way of being in the world. However, there was a nine-month interval when I stopped keeping any kind of diary because I was too afraid to trust in the present. Death, the future-thief, had stolen my firstborn and stopped me in my tracks. If I had written, this is what I might have said, imagined in real-time for my daughter or granddaughter to read and translate:

9 February 2021

I have become accustomed to studying the doctor or nurse's face before turning my gaze toward the display screen of an ultrasound. This time, at the start of a brave new year, the consultant has offered me a very early scan but can't promise that he will see anything.

He repeats the familiar movement of a probe back and forth across my slime-covered belly. Then I watch his Covid mask crease with a big smile and he says, slowly but confidently, "Jemma, I can see two birth sacks". It takes me a moment to realise what this means. I allow myself to look fully at the grainy etching on the monitor, appearing like a child's brass rubbing on a tree trunk.

For the rest of the morning, I am alone with a secret shared only between the doctor, myself and the twins' elder brother who surely made this all happen. To steady myself from shock, I buy a large fudge donut from the hospital canteen and devour it back inside the privacy of my car. This will become a ritual reward as scans become more frequent and my appetite insatiable. I dust sugar from my fingertips onto my coat and turn the key in the ignition. The road back home is icy and I grip the steering wheel like three lives depend on it. I picture how I will tell their father the news. As I do so, the road turns into Holyrood Park and winter sunlight bounces off the peaks of Salisbury Crags up to my righthand side – ancient rock made of deep time. Below, inside a car travelling through a city that has never looked more beautiful, my body carries the response to questions I have been searching for. This is the future in twin track. And the biggest adventure of my life is just beginning.

SPIDER MOTHER

Kerri ní Dochartaigh

In the very early weeks of motherhood – foggy, milky, weepy – I read a post on Instagram that changed the way I moved through the world. It was something along the lines of –

No matter where you go, no matter for how long, there will now always be an invisible thread pulling you back.

I've tried, to no avail, to find this post again – just to get the wording right – but to be honest I'm not sure that part really matters. It was really just about the way the words made me feel.

The way they made me see myself as a spider, almost instantaneously.

Insect mother in place of human mother.

Eight legs in place of two.

Making my way through life with a wee silken parachute that now had a pouch sewn in; a place that, if missing my spider baby, I was to assume, would leave me feeling like half a spider. A shadow of my former black, many-legged, furry self. And to be fair, this is not a million miles from the truth in many odd, somewhat unmappable ways.

*

My child was conceived and born during Covid lockdowns.

In Ireland, for much of this time-period, we had amongst – if not the *actual* – strictest lockdown conditions worldwide.

Our maternity restrictions were more extreme than anywhere else I have heard of. The trauma left over from birth (and the run up and aftermath) still runs incredibly deep, for many, many people.

To be so steeped in fear – the fear of things unknown; the fear of an invisible virus; the fear of death; the fear of loss – at a time when my energy should have been able to be placed on things entirely different – may haunt me always. I am not sure – hopeful though I may be – that this sense of having missed out on something central to the experience of being pregnant will ever leave me.

When I fell pregnant, I had experienced the longest period of my adult life in one single place, having spent years defining who I was by the places where I went. By the journeys I made, mostly solo, across the surface of our achingly beautiful, eternally startling planetary home. I was always running – from people, places, situations – and the only thing that made any of my tricky, triggering past feel far enough away that I stood a chance of making it through – was being alone in spaces I had never before set eyes on. I'm a stickler for an 'aul cliché', as they say, and I found *myself* through finding *places*.

The ways that places I had never even heard of, let alone been in, managed to hold me – in all my chaotic, grieving, traumatised pain – did something to the inside parts of me that I might spend a lifetime trying to verbalise. I tried to make a start on mapping this all, my relationship with place, in my first book, but I found that writing about it made me desire even more places, even more of the time.

More, more, more.

What is it about us, about me, that is always willing things away, in search of the next, the next, the next?

Anyhow, suffice to say – as the years of my pre-pandemic adulthood unfurled, fern-like – I gave myself over to the want in me, the need. The hunger to go, go, go. I learned, eventually though, to stop running. I finally put down roots. I wrote about it, how I could feel the shift away from encountering place in a needy way, towards experiencing it in an exploratory way. I began craving a deeper sense of immersion: I wanted to stay still in places. Even then I was craving new places, it must be said. I still wanted my life to be full of freshness, excitement, sensory overload – but I hoped to be less in need of *go go going*.

I planned to go somewhere, many somewheres in fact, for prolonged periods of time. To *live there* for the time I was there, I suppose. I wanted, I wrote in my journal – that winter before the pandemic properly reached us here in Ireland – to travel somewhere and *be*. To simply sit there, in all those places, and read. To light a candle and write, write, write. To lie in an overgrown garden and drink coffee. To watch the bees land on various different flowers: poppies (purple ones, double-headed ones, soft peach Icelandic ones); borage (blue and white both); cornflowers (all the colours, their pastel perfection); love-in-a-mist (there must be at least a single white amongst the blue) and corncockles (white, white, white.)

I wanted to travel, still, perhaps more than I ever had before, but I wanted to do it differently. My body – all its seen and unseen parts – was hungering, for the very first time, for *less.*

Places were still calling to me, but I knew the healing they could offer me would work differently if I simply learned to stay.

It is kind of tricky to unravel why this is exactly: age, experience, falling in love, finding a home in myself?

Perhaps all of these led to my knowing that what I really needed to do was stay.

To stop awhile.

To rest.

To give myself over to the world – all her stillness, all her softness, all her secrets.

Just before the pandemic arrived, I'd been making a way in towards the creature of my second book. I could smell her, her wild abandon. I knew I would write about place, again, but this time I would make it stranger, eerier. This time I would make it wilder … I would write about learning *to be still.*

Within a week of sending off the proposal for this unusual book, with its fiercely strange little topics – isolation, loneliness, staying in one place for long periods of time – the whole world locked down. Every single one of us was asked to stay put. All travel ceased. Within a handful of months, I was carrying my first child.

A child I had been told I would never be able to have.

A vital part of my story about travel has always been about making peace with not having this child.

A child I dreamed about most nights of my adult life.

A child who, although not *there* in the way we have come to mean when we speak of *presence*, nonetheless made me feel so much less alone as I travelled the world, solo, through my twenties and long into my thirties.

A child I could feel tucked up in my navy wool jacket, watching the Aurora Borealis dance above the water in Reykjavik the year I turned thirty, cars honking in time with the geese.

A child I had watched pulling the pale pink blossom off the trees in the Edinburgh Botanic Gardens. Howling with joy as they ran through Samhain trees, hung with strings of light, carrying their wee watercolour lantern, made at kindergarten, through a Glasgow community garden.

A child who had swum in a muddy river in India, safe in my arms, singing.

A child who had called me, called me, called me; further, further still, along the coastal paths of the Lizard peninsula in Cornwall; small creamy arms full of equally creamy meadowsweet.

It all got very tangled up for me: the not-ever-coming child and the not-ever-stopping traversing of this exquisite earth. I saw my future as one in which the only responsibilities, the only demands on my time, the only ties to my body, were all purely my own. Because I saw no other person in that future – especially not a small one who would need me all day every day from the moment they arrived – I saw a very particular future held for me on the path ahead. Because that wee one was not coming, I needed to make sure I soaked up every ounce of this planet I possibly could, in the hope that – through doing so – I might keep the unspeakable grief at bay.

And then they came, you see. That not-ever-coming-child *came*. The child who I had carried, hidden inside me, everywhere I had travelled for well over a decade before they finally made their way into my grateful, 'geriatric' womb. And when they did, the whole planet changed colour and shape entirely. This earth, one I had grown to feel I knew, somehow, more intimately, even, than I knew my own body, became utterly unrecognisable.

How does a person, a woman, a mother, make their way through a world they can no longer read?

When our surroundings become unmappable, how are we expected to carry on?

I was diagnosed in my third trimester with perinatal depression. The life I had led until that point had left me extremely vulnerable to it, but still I found myself shocked. This was what I had wanted my whole entire life, and now I spent my days weeping, wracked with anxiety and deeply rooted fear.

What exactly was I supposed to do to make all the colours come back?

*

That wee spider child made their way earth-bound. And we stayed put, and the colour drained away even further. And along with the side effects of the depression, there were the side effects of a love I could never have even nearly imagined. A frightfully wild cocktail indeed.

Life with a newborn can anyway look very small, quiet; the map of your days a direct replica of the space in which the feeding & winding, crying & sleeping (or not) fall into their own ebb and flow. When you add, into this tiny world, a lockdown, PND, and a baby who struggled to eat or sleep, the map becomes so small that even Alice with her looking glass would find herself lost in wholly dangerous ways.

We went absolutely nowhere, aside from the doctor's, the pharmacy, and an excruciatingly heartbreaking weigh-in centre, temporarily housed on the site of one of the worst mother and baby homes in Ireland.

I could not take my spider baby out of that silken pouch for even a moment before he howled so sorely, he turned blue. The midwife had called him an attachment baby; told me that in Germany they called them *lily babies*, but I was too tired to ask her why. I could not pee without him attached to me. He only calmed when the surfaces of our (apparently) separate skins were in full contact. We were locked in a co-dependent orbit, me and this person I had only just met. I tried to imagine ever going anywhere at all; seeing a place in this world that I had never before seen, and I bawled even louder than the soft furry body attached to my own. I was lost. I was without a map. I felt held in a way I was deeply troubled by. I was, instead of untethered, *tethered*, and I was not sure how I would ever get myself free again.

*

This is being talked about an awful lot more these last few years than it was when I began my matrescence journey, and for that my heart is very glad. By *this*, I mean the fact that (m)othering can be beautiful & harrowing, terrifying & healing all in one go. By *this*, I mean that we can want to be with our small people all the time but also want to be alone again, free from all these invisible ropes of caregiving within late-stage capitalism. That we can want to book ourselves an open ticket to anywhere, even the next village over from our own, without having to deal with the non-stop guilt and grief that can come hand in hand with being apart from the person you are raising.

Sometimes we lose ourselves on this journey in ways that all the travel of all the life that came before could never prepare us for. And sometimes, somehow – despite the brambles and shadowy tree stumps we have come to take as the boundaries of our new world – we find the path again. And fuck me, is that the most beautiful thing we might ever imagine.

Slowly, with the support of a very attentive partner, beautiful friends, and a cracking therapist, I started to make my way back up from the underworld. I began, tentatively, to imagine a life, again, that somewhat resembled the one I'd spent almost two decades creating for myself. A life of places; of travel; of joy.

A life where I would start, once more, to feel like *me*.

There is quite a huge part of me that feels I need to tell you –

I love my child so much, I am so unspeakably grateful, I would go through this all again in an instant just to have him

– but I have to trust that you will not judge me, either way. That you will not judge *us*.

I have to trust that you will listen to mothers; you will hold them close; you will trust them.

*

Something quite unexpected happened in the aftermath of that journey with PND, and I am still too early into feeling okay to properly get to grips with it. But I want, at least in a small way here, to try.

This is how it looked, my travelling towards recovery. I started, instead of going places alone, going with my spider baby. He was still so small, so new, so vulnerable, and in many ways, I was too. And so, we started small. We were living, back then, in a tiny Cornish village, to which we had moved in an attempt to make me feel like me again. The pandemic had wreaked havoc with maternal mental health support in Ireland, and we hoped that relocating somewhere new, by the sea, and crucially with access to the NHS, might be the answer to our increasingly worrying situation. So two months to the day after he started to crawl, at seven months old, we moved with our spider baby to the Lizard peninsula.

And we began to take him places, which – for a pandemic baby – felt wilder than I can really word …

We began with quiet places. We went at ungodly hours; such is the timetable of a non-sleeping mama and baby. We prepared for our daytrips to the fishing village of Newlyn as though we were going away for a week in London. I paid special attention to what books I was feeling drawn to bring, as I always used to do for a solo trip, knowing full well I would not have a single chance to open them. I planned where we would get our take-away coffee, and where I would sit to drink it, if nursing needs allowed. I dreamed of what treasure the single charity shop might offer me as though I were going to the Stoke Newington charity shops for the day. I brought swimming gear, knowing that the thing that returns me most to myself is the sea, swimming in the sea somewhere to which I have travelled. It somehow had stopped mattering that the journey was only in our car and lasted forty minutes on a good traffic day.

*

We branched out, once the baby and I turned one, and I felt brave enough to return to Ireland, to try to make peace with the place it had all began. We travelled, just as we had in Cornwall, on the island. Just as I had done, alone, for many years, I set up my tent, bought strawberries from the market in Moville, and listened to a babbling river and the sound of the crows going home for the night. This time there was a small, walking babe in the tent, too.

We went to the West of Ireland, and I watched poppies sway in the wild winds of County Clare, as my spider baby planted potatoes for the first time, with an Airbnb host who would become like a granny to him, a mother to me.

I had never set foot in a garden quite like that one before.

I never have since.

It feels from another time, another place.

I was held by its timeless, placeless beauty in ways I never really knew a place could hold a person.

Even after two decades spent thinking, writing, dreaming about *place* – this garden took me by the hand and led me back.

Back, not to a place as such, but to a person.

Back to someone I was fairly sure I had lost forever.

She gave me borage, blue as the Atlantic: for courage.

A wall of yellow fennel, her exquisite, tangible message: *Remember Joy.*

And what about those poppies, swaying in those westerly winds?

Beauty lives here still, she said, *here in this place beyond your recognition.*

Hope, too, held within this seed-head, a future being sown by your own capable hands.

SPIDER MOTHER

That garden was a woman, that woman was a mother.

That garden was a mother, and I could be, too.

I began to realise I was making my way to a new – incredibly new, in fact – place. One I had never before set eyes on. And it felt glorious, delicious beyond all words.

On that trip, I was alone for a week, more or less, for the very first time with my son, aside from the hour before bed when my partner returned from a course. The safety net of his spider father, my silken parachute, gone. Our host, that beautiful artist with that wild garden overlooking the even wilder Atlantic, knew well what we were doing; knew the person I was trying to coax back into being. So she danced around us, delicately, sometimes winding her silk in close to us two, me and that spider baby I was away with, having begun to make my way through the fog. Sometimes she left us with the quiet of the rain hammering the roof of her studio, singing down to us, from above, so we knew she was there. But distant enough that I could find my own way.

Who am I, now I know I can never go back to who I was before?

Now I know I will perhaps never feel the same way about travel, about leaving home on my own, ever again.

Who am I, having been so close to the edge, closer than ever before, but having found my way back?

*

Nearing the end of that trip, my partner came back from his course for the weekend. The artist invited me upstairs from our rented space, into her art studio. I hadn't done something like that in my motherhood journey to that point – been so close to my baby but left him. Through the wooden floor I could hear him crying, desperate for me, for my body, for my milk, for my everything. I could hear his father singing to him, dancing with him, playing with him, and eventually taking him out into that garden; the one I am confident saved my life. We looked out, the artist and me, over the hills of Fanore. She pointed out the curves, those that she simply cannot get out of her work. The colours, the flowers, the sea, the memories of her motherhood journey – much more grief-filled than my own – are all so much a part of that place for her that she needs to be there to make her work. I had known the artist as a free woman who travelled constantly, and to hear this side to her work, this need to stay put sometimes, made me weep. At first quietly, then so loudly I could have almost become embarrassed in a different setting. I could feel, for the first time since pregnancy, things begin to fall into place. To settle, to quieten, to be at peace.

No matter where you go, no matter for how long, there will now always be an invisible thread pulling you back.

There is so much focus on the baby.

We need to hold the mother too.

When a person becomes a mother, they might not have quite realised that they will meet two new people that day: their baby, and the person *they themselves* have now become.

And maybe that invisible thread is actually pulling us back to the *second* one.

MIDDER

Roseanne Watt

According to an Orcadian folktale, the Northern Isles and the Faroe Islands were formed from the fallen teeth of a dying sea serpent: Muckle Mester Stoor Worm, the father of all sea dragons. The story is stappit-fu[16] with classic folktale archetypes: an idle crofter's son, a king facing a terrible choice, a cunning spaeman,[17] as well as a fair few sacrificial virgins. And, as in any folktale worth its salt, it is the fool character of Assipattel, the daydreamer amongst the ashes, always imagining himself the hero of his own dreamt-up stories, who saves his island from the Stoor Worm's jaws. This is something I have noticed, with only a coarn[18] of covetous rivalry, about the Orcadians' folktales: they tend more towards the epic than those found in Shetland.[19]

Assipattel felled the Stoor Worm by sailing a small boat into the monster's yawning mouth, wherein he set its liver ablaze with a flaming peat brought from the hearth of his beloved fireplace,

16   stuffed; full

17   a fortune-teller, prophet, wizard

18   a small quantity

19   To give a delightful example of this contrast, in Shetland, 'Essipattel' appears as a *Cinderella* character, whose fairy godmother takes the form of a magical 'blue yowe' (blue ewe).

causing the Stoor Worm to writhe and retch. With each elska-cry,[20] the Stoor Worm's teeth scattered across the North Sea, creating in turn three archipelagos: first Orkney, then Shetland, and lastly the Faroe Islands. Another thrash dislodged that fearsome forked tongue, which flew right over the fjords and mountains of Norway and Sweden, landing with such force it created the Baltic Sea. Finally, the Stoor Worm's burning body curled up into a tight black knot and became the island of Iceland, whose landscape of geysers and volcanoes suggests that the body of the monster still smoulders to this day.

Once, I may have told you how I felt a certain resonance with Assipattle's arc: that son of a crofter who lived at the edge of the kingdom, dreaming himself into the centre of his world. It is a lovely sentiment, is it not? Still, these days I fear there might be more of the sea serpent in me. Something about that dreadful tongue, submerged in seawater; something about old, hot pain buried deep below the surface of things. How the teeth of these stories have sunk deep in my skin, stayed with me through all my journeys between South and North.

*

A few years ago, a family friend found an old video tape of my great-grandmother, who we all called Auld Mam, telling stories of our family's lore. We gathered to watch it in the same room where the recording was made, in the ben end of my grandmother's house.

In the tape, Auld Mam recounts tales that featured the peculiar, prophetic gifts of her mother, my great-great-grandmother, who everyone referred to affectionately as Midder. Auld Mam begins with a story during the First World War, where Midder dreamed

20   death-cry

she saw her stepson's ship torpedoed by a German U-Boat, his living body in the water, gripping onto a piece of wood alongside three other crewmates. Three times she saw him lose consciousness, his grip slackening; three times she woke, crying out his name – Robbie – into the darkness, warning him he was in the water, to hold on, help was near. When Robbie returned to Shetland, he told her that his ship had indeed been torpedoed, and that he'd heard her; her voice had woken him from the brink of drowning three separate times, until an American liner rescued them from the water.

Auld Mam tells these stories in English. I've noticed this happening before when interviewing older generations of Shetlanders. How a camera or microphone somehow commands that they 'speak properly', as many of them would devastatingly phrase it. English calcifies her tongue. Shaetlan lurks below her syntax, sometimes slipping to the surface. Grannie thinks her versions of the stories are wrong. The pacing is off; the details aren't quite right.

Auld Mam is ninety-six years old in the recording. Her voice is silty with age. In the breath between one tale and another, she stops to declare bluntly: "An I hae no stories o my ain. It wis aa joost hard wark."

*

At the sokken[21] between lockdowns during the Covid-19 pandemic, my boyfriend and I moved back 'home' to Shetland. I have put that tricky word in quotation marks for good reason, having learned something of the difference between moving back and moving home in the years since.

21   the time of slack water between the last of the ebb and the first of the flood

The move itself wasn't exactly intentional. In our minds, we had only returned for an extended holiday, to see longed-for family members and friends in the flesh, instead of in pixels. We loved Edinburgh, the city we had lived in for the last decade, and had no firm plans to move away, but there are times when history intervenes and makes these decisions for you.

There was also no denying that Shetland had pulled on both of us from the moment we'd left it, and more so in those fretful days of the first lockdown. Many islanders will tell you about that feeling, and we were no less tethered by it. We had always been compass needles, the pair of us, pointing north.

Moving back had crept up on us like a flood tide, but as it did, a plan for the future began to emerge: when it was safe enough, we would cancel our lease in Edinburgh and get our things moved to Shetland, then stay with my boyfriend's parents in the northern-most isle of Unst, until we could find a place of our own. We knew none of this would be easy. The housing stock in the islands is critically low, with rentals 'as rare as hens' teeth', as one post put it in a local housing Facebook group. Or maybe sea-serpent's teeth.

Luckily (for luck was indeed a large force at play here), after nearly a decade of scraping our savings together, we reckoned we were finally in the position to actually buy a place of our own. We dreamed of finding a house somewhere rural, preferably north of Lerwick; not too far from the ferry terminal to Yell and Unst, nor too far from my own family and our friends who lived in the south-end of the isles. Aside from that, my only other requirement was that a beach remained within reasonable walking distance. In my imaginings of this place, I could see myself combing some exposed rib of shoreline, doused in ruckly[22] after-storm light of the kind that acted on my soul like a good, old ache.

22   uneven, as a surface

*

Shortly after we'd ended the lease on our Edinburgh flat, articles started to emerge in national newspapers that documented an apparent exodus taking place across the country. Driven stir-crazy by multiple lockdowns, people who lived in the urban centres of the UK had become starkly aware of the exact square footage of their lot in life. For those who owned their homes outright, calculations were being made: they could sell their flats and semi-detached townhouses for tens of thousands more than what an entire detached house cost in rural areas. A country-wide escape to the country.

In Shetland, we started to hear crazy tales of houses going for as high as thirty per cent above the asking price, sold without ever having been viewed by the buyer, within hours of having been listed on the market. Whilst we suspected much of this was just spik,[23] there did appear to be some truth that the rural houses were being snapped up for well above their asking prices. We soon made the dismal calculation that to stand any chance of matching the current rates of deposits, we would need to spend another decade saving every penny we had.

Had I Midder's gifts, I might have foreseen the predicament we were about to find ourselves in. Even without them, I wasn't surprised things were turning out in such a way. Precarity runs like a fault-line through Shetland's history. For me, this was simply another chapter in the same story the women in my family had been telling for generations.

*

23   rumours, hearsay

There was a short period of time where my Grannie lived in Edinburgh; in a flat on 55 Warrender Park Road, in the leafy neighbourhood of Marchmont. Her father, my great-grandfather, had died when she was only four years old, which left Auld Mam fending for the family as a single mother. She went where the work was; first as a maid in a Lerwick townhouse, then as a cook and housekeeper to four students in Edinburgh. In later years, she followed the fish roads between Scalloway and Great Yarmouth as a herring lass.

My grandmother has fond memories of their time in Edinburgh, though it's not in her nature to tell stories without some lining of hope or humour in them. A particular favourite from her time in Auld Reekie goes like this: she was once asked by her teacher at the Sciennes School to recite some poetry, but the only verse my grandmother had committed to memory was a Shaetlan poem by James Stout Angus called 'The Kittiwake'. So be it; she stood up and delivered this lilting poem in her native language aloud to the class.

"Now wasn't that marvellous, children?" Her teacher remarked afterwards. "That was a poem *in the Gaelic*."

*

In the summer of 1939, Auld Mam took the family back home to Shetland for the holidays, sailing from Leith Docks on the *Earl of Zetland*. The sea, according to my Grannie, was like a mirror, thick with the black reflections of night and the moon's sunken light.

My Grannie and her siblings were playing a game of picky on the deck, when suddenly the water beside the steamer began to churn, disturbed by something moving just beneath the surface. A vast shadow began to emerge from the depths, and my Grannie ran from the railings in terror, believing she was witness to the Devil himself rising out of the black water. She kept her distance, until she heard an incredulous voice naming the entity for what it really was: a German U-Boat.

A few weeks later, on the day before they were all due to travel back to Edinburgh, a telegram arrived from a relative named Jockie; a captain in the royal navy. The body of his message contained only four words:

STAY PUT. WAR IMMINENT.

Auld Mam did not believe Jockie's telegram at first, and threatened to put them all on the steamer regardless. She finally relented when her cousin brought up the risk that, if there was a war coming, the bairns might be taken from her in Edinburgh and sent to the safety of the Scottish countryside.

Jockie's prophecy came true: the next day war was indeed declared. They stayed. Weeks turned into months, months turned into years, and without really getting to decide it, they had moved back home, never returning to Edinburgh again.

For a while they lived on the family croft at Burland with Midder, until the death of my great-great grandfather passed its ownership into the hands of his eldest son, who had a young family of his own to shelter. A house in Scalloway called Sea View came up for rent, and Auld Mam wrote to apply for it. The story goes that the man who owned Sea View didn't want to labour over the decision of who his next tenants would be; they would select them from the first letter they opened. By sheer luck, that letter was Auld Mam's.

When I asked my Grannie what happened to the things they left behind in Edinburgh, she just shrugged. "I doot dere wisna muckle tae recover."

*

A pain surfaced in the lower left side of my back, just below the ribcage. Like most basic millennial women of the pandemic, I was sixteen days deep into a Yoga With Adriene thirty-day challenge. I named the pain Pulled Muscle, managed to reach day twenty-seven before admitting defeat. Three months went by, and the pain grew to be a set of teeth, clamped around my left hip.

It was only when I started pissing bright red blood that I finally began to think of phoning the doctor. It happened the morning after a long hike with friends. I had joined them even though my body was saying a clear "no" to any kind of exertion. I told myself I could push through it; that it was, in fact, good and right to do so. Since puberty, my body had always harboured some degree of pain. I'd learned to dismiss it. I hadn't recognised this new one for what it was: a premonition; the first, dark call of warning.

*

My Mam is Irish. She grew up in Dublin and studied nursing in London, before she moved permanently up north. The local term for people like her is 'sooth-moother'. Another tricky word. It means, literally, a person who has arrived in Shetland via the south mouth of the Lerwick harbour, but also wryly nods towards a person who does not speak the native language. Whenever I've heard it used, it has always sounded benign to my ears; a statement of fact, rather than some value-judgement upon a person's right to reside here, or snide comment on the way they speak. Recently, however, there have been articles and comments by such incomers in the local newspapers, expressing their discomfort with the word, and I find myself caught between the two points of view: the first which insists that only native speakers get to decide what the words of their language really mean; the second which recoils at the prospect of making anyone feel like they don't get to truly belong here.

My mother first came to Shetland on a short holiday, after completing her nursing training in London. When asked what it was that made her come back and stay here, taking on the posts of district nurse and midwife, she will tell you it was the simple fact that no one felt the need to lock their doors in Shetland. It was a level of safety, of faith in your community, which she had never known in the cities of her birth or studies. That is a crucial thing, I think, when it comes to this idea of islands and escape. What is it, precisely, that you're escaping from? And what do you think you're escaping to?

*

The pain began to consume me. The parameters of my travels could be measured in the distance between the back bedroom and the toilet. My skin turned a stony shade of grey. I missed the sea. If I managed to write anything, it came out fragmented. Scattered teeth. Skerries of verse. Archipelagic paragraphs. A sea of white space.

*

The GP in Unst phoned to tell me my blood results had come back abnormal. A marker called CA125 was three times higher than it should be. After all this time, someone had found a way to get my blood to tell the story of what my body was going through. The word 'endometriosis' surfaced like some ancient sea creature; a condition I had been told, many years ago, I could not possibly have.

I was referred to the hospital in Lerwick, and met with a gynaecologist who recast some doubt on the endometriosis theory. Some of the symptoms I was experiencing just didn't seem to fit. Still, the blood results puzzled her enough to arrange a meeting with a specialist. There's that luck, again. There are only two hundred endometriosis specialists in the entirety of the UK. Somehow, our hospital has one visiting every other month. I told him my symptoms, and he surmised there was a sixty per cent chance they were being caused by endometriosis. Far from certain, but the promise of an answer was not yet slockit.[24] A diagnostic laparoscopy was organised for me.

*

What do you do in a body that can't travel?

You move across landscapes of words and images. You journey with your mind. For me, this meant wandering through my boyfriend's mother's shelves of Shetland books. In our room, I had pinned a map of Shetland on the wall, and every time I came across a folktale which was set in a particular part of the Isles, I stuck a red pin in that place on the map. It wasn't long before the length and breadth of the archipelago was spotted with the petechiae of its stories.

Meanwhile, my search history became a litany to the minutiae of endometriosis. I found little in the way of groundbreaking scientific research, despite the disease affecting an estimated one-in-ten women. Too spent to summon any kind of righteous female rage on the matter, I instead consumed patient anecdotes posted on forums and subreddits, and stared at photographs of the disease's lesions and tumours. They looked to me like the stenloopens[25] of anenomes found on exposed rocks at low tide. Were such creaturely lesions lurking inside me, too?

24   extinguished, a light which has gone out
25   blood-blisters

I prepared myself for the very real possibility that the surgeons would cut me open and find nothing to explain my agony. I researched differential diagnoses, just in case. In the dense, unforgiving terrain of medical language, I came to relish instants where things were named after natural phenomena: bile lake, string of pearls, cherry angioma, island sign, the little moon in the heart. I learned that blood is the body's way of recreating the primordial ocean of our single-celled origins, which in turn made me think of another Orcadian epic: the battle of the Sea Mither[26] and Teran, the spirits of summer and winter, whose elemental clashes for jurisdiction over the isles brought about the cycle of the seasons. In the story, it is Sea Mither who was said to bring life and vitality to the waters surrounding the Northern Isles, which I have taken to mean that the great artery of the Gulf Stream is the product of her labour.

*

It eventually occurred to me that ChatGPT might be able to divulge even more of these small, gratifying moments of familiarity in that wide sea of medical jargon. And it did, at first. I soon came to realise, however, that most of the terminology it suggested had been brazenly made up; its eagerness to provide an answer was more important than those answers being actually factual. I felt glad, in that moment, that ChatGPT was not yet my doctor.

Still, I was startled to find it had invented the name of a condition I did not know I'd needed the words for:

Solsticialgia: the first onset of pain in a chronic medical condition, named after the solstice, which marks the transition from one season to another. (Etymology: 'Solstice' meaning 'sun stands still,' and 'algia' meaning "pain.")

26 In Shetland, her name is Sea Midder.

*

What do you do in a body that can't move you back into belonging?

You inhabit its language. You enter its new seasons and weather its storms. You tell the stories of the things that hurt, and hope you don't lose yourself in them.

*

The expression 'tae ging tae ta da ebb'[27] means to be so destitute that you survive from the shoreline; off of wylks, limpets and waar,[28] off of finsters[29] along the banks.[30] Historically, it was often women with no living husband or land to their name, whether by circumstance or stigma, who were forced to walk the ebb. It was seen as the lowest form of livelihood, betrayed in the dismally ironic insistence of proverbs such as 'a shillin oot o da wylk-ebb is as bricht as een oot o da Hooses o Parliament.'[31]

No one should face such utter deprivation, and it is a cruel system of governance that allows for such a thing to happen. I try to find some small, bleak mercy in how, where land tenure and wage economies failed them, the ebb was a place that could hold these folk. Owned by no one, the sea takes possession of the dispossessed.

27 to go to the ebb. The ebb is that place on a beach which is revealed by the ebbing tide.

28 a kind of seaweed

29 a discovery, a good find

30 the sea cliffs

31 a shilling from gathering whelks is as bright as one from the Houses of Parliament.

*

I would like to tell you this story ends happily. They found endometriosis. I was cured. I recovered my mobility. My partner and I found a house beside the sea, near our family and friends. There was no more illness and no more loss. The truth is, of course, more complicated than that.

Yes, I woke to the surgeon telling me they'd found both endometriosis lesions and adhesions. Thick loops of scar tissue were slung across my abdominal organs, wrapping them together in a tight bind. She'd burned the lesions away; cut my organs free from the adhesions. I would walk upright again, in time. My periods would arrive without any kind of dreadful fanfare.

The pain in my left side remained unchanged, though its parameters have become less muddied by those other infiltrations. I had expected this. Knowing now the different dimensions of pain I was harbouring, I realised this one had always been different. It did not recede with heat, nor wax and wane throughout the month's cycle. It was always there, a constant ache, worse on some days than others. Over time, it spread down my left leg, all the way to my ankle. A dynamic, travelling pain. Even now, I am still getting used to the ebb-like boundaries of my body, never sure if the tide of a flare up is coming in or rushing out.

We bought a flat in Lerwick, the only kind of accommodation that had remained stable in price, being far from the mainlanders' imagined ideal of island living. In the stress of mortgage negotiations and admin, I laid an aamos[32] on my witchiest friend, a borrowing of her luck. And we do count ourselves lucky.

From our sitting-room window, I can see the harbour. I can watch the sea in all her moods, even if I cannot reach her. I wait

32   a gift promised in secret for the fortunate outcome of a situation

for the North Boat to make its nightly pilgrimage. Listen for the organ-bellow horns of the larger cruise ships. On clear days, I can see the spidery spectres of the Viking Energy Wind Farm taking form in the hills of Da Lang Kames, and feel something like grief and something like fear take root.

*

Here is another of Midder's premonitions. My Grannie would hear her, muttering this phrase over and over again, as she swept ash and dead embers from the hearth:

"Da famine will start i da sea first."

*

I spent the weeks of convalescence flicking through Shetland dictionaries, in search of some articulation of this wild new landscape which English could not offer me. In the Christie-Johnsons' dictionary, I came across the word 'life-tinkin'; a word for recovery, though its literal English cognate is 'life-thinking'.

Here it was, my way through the body's wilderness: a word which bypassed entirely the idea of 'recovery', with its suggestion that we can endure times of pain, or illness, or loss, and never find ourselves irrevocably transformed by the experience. But there are some things which cannot go back to normal, and some things that shouldn't, and some things which must be left behind.

Life-tinkin is a different proposition. It reads like an instruction: turn your thoughts towards life, my midder tongue tells me, whatever that might mean for you.

A BARREN TRANSLATION

Alison Phipps

"Spontan Abort"[33]

There is a female creature who hides in her womb unborn children

And although the infants are voiceless they cry out across the waves

Of the sea

And over the whole earth to whomever they wish

And people who are not present and even deaf people can hear them.

The female creature is a letter

And the infants she carries are the letters of the alphabet:

Although voiceless they can speak to those far away,

---

33   On 5th April 1999, Easter Day, while travelling in Germany, on the anniversary of her paternal Grandmother's birthday, she had what she was told was a 'spontan abort'. This was only known of in German. In English, despite the efforts of translation there is no medical record. There are the records of subsequent operations but nothing accurate is recorded, is publicly to be known. In order to make sense of the knowledge that became no knowledge at all she learned to order the fragments of what she gradually came to know she knew, into letters, and into poetry and into ways of knowing, until the trauma of missed translation and of missed carrying resolved, out of translation and in the language of the trauma.

She has no children.

THERE SHE GOES

To whomever they wish whereas if someone happens to be
Standing right next to the reader he will not hear.

Antiphanes Sappho

Fragments
Sappho.
Fragments.
Life.
In fragments.

When the fragments are voiced, the sound pierces the membranes of memory and moment.

Did Sappho travel? What do I know of the women on Lesbos a couple of thousand years ago? Did she have children? Did her body travel in the way her mind did? Did she travel across the bodies she loved or did she just long for them? What do we know? These are not the questions that detain me. That she was a poet of longing. That is what matters when longing to move. When longing to not be in the pain of a present. When longing is for what is absent.

Where is my infant – lost in the fragments of the letters of the alphabet. First known in the bleeding, in the crying out over sea and over earth. Why even the deaf heard the tearing of life from the womb.

The female creature is a doctor.

She has a pen in place of a scalpel.

Her letters are not my mother's tongue, but now in the tongue for this moment of mothering, they write out the life and the death in the same instance. "Spontan abort".

] But …

] I am not …

Dead you will lie and never memory of you
Will there be nor desire into the after time – for you do not
share in the roses of Pieria, but invisible too in Hades' house
you will go your way among the dim shapes. Having been
breathed out. (55)[34]

The unborn child is no longer hidden in the womb.

The child, no longer a child, but a dead foetus now, is in a small plastic tupperware pot, loaned by a friend,

preserved in pure ethanol.

Having been breathed out.

Science insists on an accurate story. I travelled for six more days. In my pack, my child, swilling around in its temporary tomb, in the tupperware womb for the dead. The letter travelled with me. A standard letter to my own doctor, from the one who did not share my mother's tongue. My story fitting neatly into boxes and typescript. Cold. Clinical. Whispering sweet nothings in Bureaucracy's hungry ear. My name, my number. My address. The code on my travel insurance. What does it mean, to in sure? The comment: "Spontan Abort". My blood pressure. It's perfect. My antibiotics. The long history of my womb – marked in German-made scars on my belly with a surgeon's ……

We walked around Florence in the Easter air. Botticelli's Venus. Mary wringing her hands at the words of the angel, blue with the cold of the greeting. I was white as chalk. *Whiter by far than an egg* (167). Noli me tangere, the words of the Risen Christ to the weeping woman. Do not touch me …… I am not ready …… *in my dripping pain*.

And everywhere, lilies.

34 Bracketed numbers here refer to Sappho's fragments, as numbered in *If Not, Winter: Fragments of Sappho*, Anne Carson, Little, Brown Book Group, 2003.

A Letter to Her Doctor from Her German Surgeon

Quit – Luxurious Woman (25D)

It's actually all a bit unclear.
There was a lot of pain.
It was Easter Day.
A tuggingdraggingrushingpulling downdraft in her body.
Down, down, down.
It brought her – miserable … to her knees.
Cloth dripping (119).

Of course, although it looks as though she had been with child for several months she didn't …….. She'd been bleeding as we do, painfully, to be sure, but that wasn't anything out of the ordinary, not for her.

She bleeds a lot.

Once before we had to undress her, and hang her legs in stirrups, and lay her on a cold table, and invite the men to see the unbearable orange fruit, mouldering away.

Of course she was too young for us to see clearly, so we had to feel our way, but she was so slender and there was no sense in trying to pluck the fruit with any more force. Already we had had to tear her.

She was so young and quiet …

biting, biting, *biting at her tender mind* (96).

With an odour of fear and, behind the cold curtain where she dressed again, hot and angry tears.

with anger spreading in the chest. (158)

virginity,

    virginity,

        where are you gone leaving me behind? No longer will I come to you. No longer will I come. (114)

So you see, this could have been just the bursting open of more rotten fruit, but I'm as sure as I can be – woman, to woman, to woman – that she has lost a child.

She was not growing it as she should, nesting it awkwardly into the corners where the flow of life hangs on too slender a thread.

Why else would she have cycled so much blood.

And there is something about her hair too … the way it hangs, its lustre.

] all

] but different

] hair

It speaks and from it I form the words I write to you to tell you. She has lost a child.

Her first and her last.

As woman to *luxurious woman* I tell you that what she knew from her body deceived her, and she did not know.

And what she now knows is that she is not.

… *with delicate woven cloths cover her up well.* (100)

With the kindest of wishes from,

a female creature,

a doctor.

(also translated).

Translated

"Hello. How are you?" Always the awkward greeting. "I'm feeling desperate, frightened, afraid. Last time they cut me open I withered for so long, so long." I don't say this. How could I say ……

"I have come to see you about something that happened whilst I was in Germany. I have a letter from the doctor. It is in German. These are my antibiotics. And in here ……" I take the blue tupperware with the foetus, eight days from the womb, from the plastic

Tesco bag. "It's in ethanol […] I thought it might be … useful."

She tells me this was thoughtful of me, resourceful, but that the laboratories cannot handle biomatter which has not been preserved their way, in their glass tubes, and that my friend's ethanol and tupperware will have contaminated the sample. It is a sample now, just for the moment, made in that word. A sample, of what? Of me, of my tongue, of a future that will never speak? She looks at it, pokes it. She doesn't know. There is the letter, but its letters are ordered in a language she doesn't understand. "Spontan Abort.". I translate. "Lit: Spontaneous Abortion" – "Miscarriage". I feel cast as clumsy. My body too gawky, too awkward to carry life or letters with grace; my spontaneity is matter out of place.

I do not swell.

I cease to be woman.

"Do you need this?" she asks. There is care in the question, but for what, for what? Eight nights I have not slept, lit awake by a slivery-blue moon in an upright plastic pot. By a contaminated sample.

Moon has set
and Pleiades: middle
night, the hour goes by,
alone I lie.
(168B)

My head shakes. She is […] *manyskilled* (190). "I'll just pour it down the …" *paingiver* (172). I know no feeling, no thought. I know no sensation and no sound. In my mouth metal flows from the biting.

] harm me
    ] crazy
    ]
    ]
    ]
    ] you, I want
    ] to suffer
] in myself I am
aware of this
]
]
]
(26)

There is no corresponding letter … nothing accurate is found for the ordering of English letters. The first lies untranslated. In my English medical file…]….]… In the wrong nest. "We will look again" she says. "We will see what we can find with an English scalpel. It will take time. But we will not need to translate. We will begin the work again."

For now, nothing is known that can travel as letter. Nothing is known.

as the sweet apple on a high branch
high on the highest branch and the apple pickers forgot –
no, not forgot: were unable to reach. (105A)

Reaching

I reach for letters, for a voice. I find nothing. His English scalpel finds nothing. There are more samples, but always nothing is known. No conclusions are reached, there is only reaching. The fragments are dark. I cannot see in the dark to put them together. In the day time the patterns I make from the pieces do not fit together. Ragged are the shapes. I come to know them well. I make them my comfortable friends until ….]… *I would not think to touch the sky with two arms* (52).

But I begin to reach out into the crack left behind, into the yawning void, into the darkness of the winter sky, with words. For the first time I think to touch the sky with words. The sky is grey, grey as the day, streaked with the stains of miscarriage.

Red, red, leaden, dead.

Kneeling in the darkness of not knowing anything but that this is where I have landed after falling, falling, falling through the crack, I reach for the small fragments which fell with me, as if they may speak and tell me my story, the story I am living but do not know.] *having been stained.(4).*

"You have …." "You have perhaps …" "you have not …" "it was a child …." "It was not a child …" "it was carried in a blue plastic tupperware, in ethanol, there was a lid … It is no more … in the knives of the drain … and outside, you knew of nothing but the samples of rain."

Reaching, reaching for something to know. *I long and seek after* (36). After what? What is after? *Sweet mother I cannot work the loom, I am broken with longing for a boy by slender Aphrodite* (1020) The longing and seeking, the reaching for a truth, for a story to live by, for something that returns me to a place of sense. Cycles return, and bleeding. These are known. But each time;

Cold sweat holds me and shaking
grips me all, greener than grass
I am and dead – or almost
I seem to me. (31)

And each time, nothing can be known.

A Second Movement of the Fragments

Letters form a letter and a second thing is known. Grief. Grief is the strangest of sifters. It shows what our true feelings are. There is no peace here. There is no knowing what to grieve.

From this crack, down, down, down draft down. No rest. Words, crack open the words. Make room in the wood for planting. Give her bulbs and a trowel and autumn curls of ground gold. May she plant for spring, plant gold, plant below my window frame, under cover of dawnlight on an October morning, for spring. For spring. Spring will come and with her violets, lilacs, swelling bulbs. Spring will swell.

Come April there are tulips. Regimented angry rows of planted red. Red, red, rage, dead.

A Pregnant Pause
And which month
is this in the
silence between us?
Is it sickness I'm
feeling or the form
of a foot?

In the loading of
meaning onto
lids and long fingers
no word soothes the spine,
there's no rhyme
telling time.

Truth is ungainly. It's
fertile and brooding,

warming the words
that are better cold-stored.

So touch me and
tell me of being and
becoming. Feed me coal
for cravings, and
then stamp out the fire.

Calm. And colours come. A planting now for peacetime, for the wearing of colour, the flash of turquoise on the ears, and purple swishing in summer with cloth of green and red and gold. Colour to live by, to learn by. Chameleon. She is a changeling, a shape-shift. Chiffon and silk, I gave you painted silk and amethyst for your ears. I gave you fragrance, beautiful, youth's dew. I gave you your beauty.

There are letters on her pages now, and her garden is tamed wild, tamed into fruit and fecundity, cornflowers welcome the foxes, and their gloves, nettles are red and campions white and pink, marigolds are, of course, gold. And always hyacinths, roses. What else is there to say? Is this healing – a colour garden wearing words? What might I tell you. For there is a restlessness and at times the life and loveliness long, long, long to swell.

Another surgeon piles his skill.

Shelter

I leave where I am and where I was and go to a place that is new. It's not far away. A train moves between mountains. I set off on my bike, on a small adventure, down the by ways, to the Bield,[35] the

---

35 A Scots word meaning 'shelter'.

haven. I sleep. I swim. I watch the water pool in my navel and dry in refracted sunlight, under an improbable bougainvillea, at high latitude, in the light of a Highland summer. In the garden there are flagstones, roughly laid out, and an apple tree crowned with roses. I have a notebook and pencil, for making plans. I am not a poet, so it does not expect to bear words that pattern the page.

Here there is peace of a kind and time is simple and there is water for washing the tired body, and air for breathing new words. Beneath my bare feet *not knowing how to pull the cloth to her ankles* (57) granite, warmed by the summer sun. *the one with violets in her lap (21); For many crowns of violets and roses (94).* The fragments gather into their first form. Letters arrange themselves into the first meaning and at last, though broken with longing, something is known.

The attitude of meditation gives way to prayer and the stories flood back that have been remembered year on year on year, of improbable birthing, of improbable execution, of improbable living after dying, stories made and told of gardens which have brought both peace and war to the earth for thousands of years.

In the Cracks
It is in the cracks that the wild things grow
bugle purpling over the stone, ox-eyes
looking fearlessly into the sun
for the light
that will one day wither their sight.
Droplets of gold vetch, stretch.

She was right first time. You are the
gardener after all, with a love
that breaks open stone, and hands too
freshly cracked
for her to touch.

Only the desperate and doubting
may press the red petal palms
and see the pollen stain their finger tips.

The membrane of memory and moment, pierced with ink, pierced with letters, pierced with the first of words. *With violets in her lap, in her lap, in her lap.*

I know the first thing, she knows of the violets. I write a letter from the stain. I know, I reach, break and long. I know that something is lost.

Like the hyacinth in the mountains that shepherd men
With their feet trample down and on the ground the purple
Flower (105B)

It is late afternoon. I walk through the grove of the shelter belt, to the Bield. Trees planted to protect against the elements; against the wind, against the fire, against the flood, against the tugging slide of mud. Halfway along the path I stop at a rotting tree stump. All is mossy, dewy banked and damp. In my hands lilacs, oil of geranium and orange. From the blue vial I pour the oil into the hollow, into the hole, into the woody crack. There are no tears. The flowers are laid down gently, laid down, down, downdraft, down. *My darling one.* (163) *I used to weave crowns (125).*

Easter Morning: Too Early
I have folded you away
in a mess of rotting tree
I have laid you down
on lilacs

I have covered you
smothered you

liberally anointed you
wept for you
dropped tears on you
filled day and night
with grief for you

I have laid you down
in scented lilacs

Milk
I long for roses
with no thorns.
For blood with
no breaking of
skin or bone.

Mostly I desire
milk, a sign
that something hungry
is born.

Something hungry is born. It brings desolation. Love weaves
round like willow, a container for grief. The milk spills, spills,
spills, salted with tears. The willow bends. And love breaks.

We find her kneading dough, waiting for it to rise, to knead
again, to fall. We find her kneading dough. There is no expectation.

She contains.

Sometimes she tears,

tears.

Always she prays,
not knowing what for.
Science closes the story.

Hers opens again.

It is not clear how this will end. Will it? Will it end?

Abay

It's not clear how this will end. And yet. There are beginnings in pasts which are present as conversations revolve around bodies of grandmothers. I am an Abay – a grandmother – to three children, living in Glasgow.

Fragments have written themselves over the years and they assemble themselves as the editor calls and the response brings these travelling writings together.

I search the archives for the dream that bore the grandchildren, and its writing. For the prose that steadies the lurching of the fragments. For the story I live by, from my own faith tradition, that gives me sisterly company and strange tales that endure the millennia.

Birth to the Barren[36]

There was a quite a build-up. In the course of three weeks I found myself travelling as a far as it is possible to travel, and then more besides. First to New Zealand, then back to Scotland for two days, and on to Syria for a week. The journey was for work, leading a Chaplains retreat in Wellington, being the first woman to deliver the annual Trinity Newman Lecture at Victoria University, standing with a dear friend at his ordination, being offered my own breath back as song in Māori, green stone hung

36 First Published in *In the Mists on the Shoreline*, edited by Christine Polhill: Wild Goose Publications, 2015, under my community name, my family name of Swinfen, the name chosen by my foster daughter. I retain the copyright.

around my neck, poetry found, shared, a journey overland and through silver ferns, followed by the endless night of a long-haul flight.

The stars over Afghanistan, the disappearing Southern Cross. And then Damascus, worship preparations in three languages, stories from Iraqi Refugees, a Celebration of the Feast of John of Damascus in the Syrian Orthodox tradition, Icons, songs, circles of deepening friendships to a lulling guitar. Rooms hidden at the back of the souk, filled with damask, cloths in every colour. Then the meal, as guests of the Syrian Orthodox Church, in a restaurant on Straight Street surrounded by armoured cars and men with AK47s, where our presence was as people of prayer and peace, as the politicians of three countries talked of the coming war.

The jet lag was quite something. I saw the sunrise every morning in Syria and would wake having turned a half circle in my sleep, my feet on my pillow.

Through all this journey I had with me a sense of reaching the end of a long period of longing for children of my own, a sense of time having run out, a weariness with the pain of it and with the ceaseless presence of this known lack and desire. I was laying this longing down, giving it up.

And alongside I was carrying terrible stories told to me by asylum seekers and by friends of appalling sexual abuse. I'd spoken with a trusted friend before I left on the journey, of the thickness of the atmosphere of pain that filled our house, where the stories had been told. I'd sat with one friend as she lost first one twin and then the second to miscarriage induced by abuse. I had written and said prayers at the crematorium as the still born child was laid to rest. Flowers from my garden, tied with string, lay on a tiny white coffin.

This, then, was the prelude to the one time that God – whoever she may be – came to me in a dream.

I was filled with pain, sweating and pushing to give birth. Blood, water, bodily smells – nothing sanitised. And there it was, a huge pomegranate, covered in the birth sack and cracking open to reveal hundreds of tiny seeds, which began to grow and flower.

I awoke, sheets and pyjamas soaking, drenched with sweat, I was weeping uncontrollably, shaking and clinging to my sleeping partner, who woke, and held me. I told him the dream. It was so vivid, beautiful, such a gift, that it didn't feel as though words like dream or nightmare were correct – vision perhaps. It felt as though something had been seen or understood. And in the stillness that follows after weeping I prayed into the dream for insight, handing it on.

And a voice came, firm, clear:

"You are not a barren woman."

ATTENTION PLEASE

Janette Ayachi

I'm twenty-two years old, in love and travelling to Italy for the first time with a man I met in a nightclub whilst studying in Stirling. Notoriously Italians make great lovers – intenso, neck nibble, spine arch, all tongue, fever, unkempt hair, flashing eyes. But R's motorbike is his real love – and quickly becomes mine too; a jet-black Suzuki that takes my breath away and dampens the space between my legs. The air is dusty, the sun is hot and his hand rests on my thigh between gear changes. Trying to understand the towns we pass through proves difficult; we move at dangerous speeds, the bike tilts close to the ground as we take sharp corners on mountainous climbs, and green cypresses sprawl above the duck-egg blue sea. That glorious act of freedom, setting one foot in front of the other, is rubbed out by acceleration and fumes. Still, what I can see of the landscape intoxicates me, as does the midday wine and hours spent kissing.

R lives in the Piedmont region where his father tends to the garden and churns wine in the basement next to a safe full of gold jewellery scraps and recycled jars of preserved fruits that pickle in the dark. We use their home in Valenza as a base as we begin to explore Italy by motorbike and train. Our journeys swerve from Piedmont to Lombardy, Veneto and Emilia Romagna, Tuscany to Umbria, and as far down as Lazio. We spend the first warm night in Florence sleeping under the stars next to a park, I dream filthy dreams and wake up with dirty feet, and later, when we cross the river Arno, I imagine what it would have been like during the Renaissance. I hum hymns and wonder who I was here, in my past life playing out visuals stored from watching Zeffirelli's *Romeo and Juliet*. If I had white chalk, I would write our names on the bridge wall, but I don't, and of course, R is eager to move on.

We arrive at the Casa di Dante, breathless and tipsy asking the divino poeta for answers, praying for them, paying for them. I touch old holy walls for feelings. But R is waiting hungry – he is always hungry – tower bells resonate and I cannot write poetry when I am being watched and waited on! I open my diary and write under the pressure of immediate capture:

Madonna; monks, saints, pomegranates, so much gold in Botticelli's vision. Seraphim is the highest angelic being of all. And in the galleries; babies with fruit and birds, women projected as more than muses, sit centre-point basking in an ethereal glow that reaches beyond the frame. Here they are not sexualised as such but remain saintly, and pure; a seismic concept of an era, Botticelli's and ours now, our sex split into the chapel jungle of virgins or whores. Even the warrior women who illuminate hope of breaking the binary are still soft, weightless and provocative – women we cannot wholly fear.

It's 5am and again, we sleep outside, near a station, waiting for a train. It reminds me of my childhood in London where my bedroom window looked out at the night trains on the Piccadilly Line; platforms have always been my playground and landscape for dreams. Not the only ones to choose this spot, nearby an old woman snores with an unbuttoned dress over her head. A girl uses her rucksack as a pillow, and another uses their neighbour's shoulder, her hands as headrests. I can't settle and by the time we're on the platform, waiting, I'm tripping out of my mind with exhaustion, hearing the repeated words over the speaker

– 'Attention please, do not cross the yellow lines' – as 'Attention please, you will not get out of here alive'.

We get on the train. R puts his arm around me and for now, it's enough. He feels the pressure to entertain, and I feel the pressure to allow myself to be entertained. Why, though? I love him, but, if you look at something long enough … it can be anything you want it to be … if you look hard, something will appear, even – especially – when there is nothing there. Love is the magic eye poster of emotions. The action of love is X-rated, but as for love – I don't rate it. Yet everyone is seemingly in love in this country; how could one not be in love? Easily, if one is used to Italy having always lived there and seeing past the surface beauty. But as the tourist brochures often flag, and in my giddy intoxication with the deliciousness of it all, I could easily believe it: the romance just geysers out of le fontane, the delight for the way things taste, in life, la Famiglia, la dolce vita. This country seems favoured to break even the most cynical.

We take a boat from Camogli to San Fruttuoso, a tiny island that only houses a monastery and one beach restaurant; I think strongly of letting him leave without me. I came here to travel, to write, instead all that occupies my head is this boy, forever before me, blocking my view. Genoa, and its Byzantinesque harbour which I've longed to see, doesn't even get its due because R is glued to me, making all the decisions.

One evening we share a caramello joint, an erotic smooch session and a romantic walk through the port piazza. We find a trattoria, sit by the window, drink beer and gaze at the women passing by. My propensity for women was present long before my relationship with R, and well, it was something that never really went away. Dusk comes quickly, lifts her skirt then salsas away, twisting across the pillars of palm trees until people, it seems to me, become self-aware chess pieces charting their strategy across tessellated squares. The trattoria is noisy and crowded. Sitting at a communal table with strangers, we lean over plates of gnocchi con pesto, endless carafes of the darkest wines, all our elbows touching, bread baskets passed down rows of pews as if there were conveyor belts in the air above our heads. The heat from the clay pizza oven has replaced the day's humidity, now that the sun has slipped from the sky. We camp out on the beach because we have drunk enough red wine to be content. And although I'm with R, I still think of women.

From Genoa to three nights in Rome with headless Romans under the two-thousand-year-old statues; always the head is first to go, then the hands. I have taken so much of this place with me, that I must leave a small part of myself behind. Apostles in glass tombs; a hurricane of thoughts in the prayer room, the scent of incense, ancient formaldehyde. Sun filters through the stained glass, blowing dust and gold around our aura, our ankles. Dreams of metamorphosis, an obsessed lover disguised as a tiger, that turns on me viciously the minute I am distracted by another, it attacks but pauses at the chance of devouring me. Rome lets its history stand still because it is a city that does not believe in burying its treasures.

On the motorbike, we drive on roads that thread through grapevines terraced on undulating slopes and pass well-adorned shop displays, gowns and gold, through dynasties and old merchants and around gladiatorial amphitheatres. I hold on to my love like I have no other love.

We eat ice cream in the park in Bergamo whilst two men shoot up in the shade; needle piercing ankle and arm, they wash away their dirt into fountains; a couple cleaning each other, the water like glass. An elderly couple press their bones into a bench and share a piece of bread, skin stained with street grime, still, they shine through their gummed smile. This is a place of annual music festivals; theatre renovations; colourful cathedrals and nuns crossing traffic lights with chained crucifixes that jingle bells; a twin city above a city; basket bicycles and market stalls, quaint and neutral, pedalling its dark into parks. Fountains sprout up where the earth needs to crack. We leave the world behind in the rearview mirror.

When we arrive in Milan, a poster tells me that the actress Asia Argento will appear as a guest in a local nightclub. I'm a fan, having watched her films with subtitles to learn the Italian language. She grew up appearing in her father's slasher films; what a way to start seeing the world. She is thrilling: disobedient, and beautiful. She's one of those actresses you sense aren't so different from the characters she plays – her storylines are intense, and she's always running. I try to convince R to take me to the nightclub, but he decides what we do in the evening. We meet his friends in another club where women dance in cages. We have a VIP table, bottles of Havana 7 on Nordic icicles in silver coolers that are so polished they morph into perfect mirrors, catching our sun-kissed hands and quick kisses. We all wear white and dance under the ultraviolet, I am the only girl and it is hot. I'm happy. I've fallen in love with not only R – despite denying me Asia, despite the doubts I've muffled – but also his country, and by giving myself to both I find in myself something that my own culture could never supply.

'Attention please, you will not get out of here alive'.

*

I carry you, child, like luggage as I travel across borders, tied to my belly like a drum – you rustle inside me like a balled and crumpled-up map of paradise, a rainbow under my skirt.

A year later, I am twenty-three and in Milan again. A gynae-cologist is mouthing 'figlia' over a blood-stained sink. Our child-to-be, probably conceived on a beach in Portofino after drinking too much, is a gift emerging from overlapping forms of intoxication. I am in love with Italy: its seascapes, melodic language, history, hearty recipes, and obsession with overflowing romance along with accompanying grand gestures; it is only R I am slowly feeling less for.

When our daughter is born, we call her Aria. Intoxication, of course, wears off. Motherhood sobers you up. After Aria is born, we visit Venice again and walk circles that ebb through those ventricle canals. With so many bridges and so many people, however, it's impossible for pushchairs; we take turns carrying with limp arms our plumb sleeping cherub child in a mandala-patterned sling.

Photos are forbidden in the heart of San Marco, life here is a sacred memory that must fade, like the archetypal marrow of bones. All veins are visible. There is no darker romance than in Venice; the gondolas twin as hearses, carrying the dead, and the exhibitionist lovers who wave at ghosts in their finest attire.

The dome of Venice is where we conceive our second daughter, Lyra, under the weight of light rain and heavy exhaustion. Although we don't marry, I become part of a family dynamic. No one's more surprised than me; my upbringing had been tough, yet here I am. I can see how I got here. On one hand, it's a solid foundation; on the other, I think of it as a pretty padlock on my front door. The choices open to me are dwindling, I had come to Italy to travel but now can't seem to turn away from it as a sort of family home. I want to fly but my wings are wet from the waters of midwifery and too sodden to lift me.

After Lyra's birth, another Scottish-Algerian-Italian baby born with a head full of curls, we journey back and forth from Edinburgh to Valenza to be near R's father as he ages. We have spoken before about moving here, to this small Piedmont village. The kitchen is glossy; the bathroom is laden with marble, the garden is plentiful, the gates are electric, the sun always shines and it is available for us to inhabit. I picture the life I want to make for myself. I will paint, sculpt, write, and drink endless bottles of *Barbera*.

*

We arrive this year to find the sunflowers dead, their heads drooping away from their eternal rows of olive trees and sleeping birds. Summer is nearly over. While R goes out to roam with his friends, I wait at the window, like a figure in a painting, but not by an Italian artist – more Edward Hopper. Someone looking out or looking in, welcoming the night and the notion that we are not alone, in being alone.

As September begins, so do the storms in Italy. Dirt blows onto the balcony in the morning. We visit R's mother's grave but bring no flowers as they're still alive from the last visit. Decades span and words lose letters. I had always thought of death as a republic, with no privileges, but walking through the graveyard I see even in this mist that the dead must submit to a hierarchy in which some families rest in marble vaults adorned with names of nobility, while others lie beneath council-funded gravestones crumbling to nothing, showing their atoms; even death dies eventually. Prayers, vows and photographs, a whole coliseum of corpses. R shows me an empty plot to the left of his mother's which is reserved for his father. Even in death, there is no escape!

My love for my children grows, while for R it fades. Seeing the same face is becoming a chore while actual chores – sparking the gas rings' blue lotuses, picking vegetables from the garden, scrubbing copper pots, washing, hanging, and folding the sharp outlines of clothes – only intensify my disenchantment. When the girls sleep in the afternoon, I take the opportunity to rediscover myself on the balcony over the garden watching the flowers and fruit absorb the sun's rays. I peer intermittently through the glass doors to check on the girls, in case they awaken to attempt an escape in my absence, perhaps because I too now want to escape. Music soothes my emptiness, and I create drawings of women in the style of Modigliani to distract myself. There is something so slow about time here, R is more demanding than ever, more than the children, and I can do no productive thinking.

Distance is all there is left. Even when I return to the UK and visit my mother and sisters, I am no longer myself, my spirit once helium is now lead. From the aeroplane the Alps sit like curdled milk above the clouds, something is always stagnating beneath; the babies are getting bigger, the conversations are getting louder and I feel the membranous layers of love for him detach from the kernel of my heart each time. I've given so much away, there's nothing left, the best of me a sacrifice on the altar of coupledom, drained by his jealousy, always obliged to give. *I miss me!* I love but feel robbed of the love I had kept for myself. His demands are a ransom I cannot afford, my heart has reached its overdraft.

Who is this person that I claim to be? A woman in a plastic portrait of a family, all smiling, linking hands like they're unbreakable. And I was the one at University who boasted about following my visions. Something inside rejects domesticity, so much so that sometimes it feels difficult to breathe. I radiate with panic as I try and fail to come to terms with not being the flâneur I'd always pictured myself to be. It would be different if I were a man, wandering the cityscape being a thing of masculine privilege and leisure, particularly in Italy, which is so governed by tradition and the church.

I try to adjust – oh, but my dreams tell me differently, and they come strong, crashing thunderous dreams, each one a warning, and I take them seriously. If only I didn't. Our relationship goes through predictable stages. We love, we turn to each other for encouragement, we argue, we hate, we rationalise, sometimes we punish and then we forgive so we can love again. Repeat. Only, the phases in which we punish each other are growing, and the need to reconcile is weakening and I have to suffer the presence of someone who has stopped talking to me.

Something has to give and eventually it does. I begin running, and R is forced to spend time alone with the children and his father. I run through fields, stop in a village when I run out of breath, find a café for an espresso, but accidentally drink two bottles of Prosecco through the afternoon, and get lost trying to return to where I started. When you open the doors to something you have caged it does not prowl out cautiously; instead, it's at your shoulder in the blink of a breath, snarling. What is this life we walk through feeding and breeding, only one day to fall into the cold latex hands of coroners? I find comfort in the supernatural element of it all, death as eventual rebirth; there's no fear then, no unknown. My mother always said it was the living, not the dead that we should be afraid of.

'Attention please, you will not get out of here alive'.

*

R has always disliked me socialising; he resents me going out and waits up to catch me coming in, frenzied in the dark, eyes searching for answers. There is so much resentment, with domesticity and freedom as the battle pieces, we can't be happy for each other. I start playing up, kissing a blonde girl in the lift at work, manifesting his fears of my infidelity. I write about it in my journals and he reads them, I never explicitly relayed the narrative, but my poems of longing and temptation were clear.

One evening he had been drinking gin, and he doesn't drink, not at home, not like that, in anger and waiting without resolution, seething underneath. The television blasts out gunshots from a videogame and I close the door. That night I sleep with Lyra, as I prefer either both or one of the kids sleeping in the bed with us, slowly masking him out to the periphery, the couch and into the abyss. I had been breastfeeding and she fell asleep wrapped up under my shoulder, her tongue still in the shape of taking milk. I too fall into a well-needed sleep, mascara itching my eyes. Until I am woken up by motion and a loud bang.

I see R hovering above me with a look of terror in his eyes. He has punched the headboard above where our baby and I had been sleeping soundly in our maternal rapture, he has punched the headboard in a last-minute swipe away from punching me.

All I needed was one flash of violence. I am not going to suffer what I grew up with, believing that violence was okay because my father loved me. I am emotionally developed enough now to know to get out. I decide to leave R and take my daughters with me but I agree to stay around until his father, sick now, dies. He doesn't know we're parting. His cancer has almost completed its work so I agree to play the part for the dying man, which is easy; I've been playing a role most of the time I've been in Italy.

When we visit, R weeps and weeps and there's one thing I can do to console him. As his father lies dying, lit by jaundice and lucid memories in an old military hospital, R and I sleep together again, both depressed, in his father's bed. A piteous heart and broken heart crashing heads, anything for a little consolation in a dark time.

Upon returning to Scotland, I find I am pregnant. What are the chances? Another child, not conceived of love at all this time, a child I cannot raise alone from birth with a four-year-old and two-year-old already. I will never forget the looks of the other girls and women in the abortion clinic, having Lyra with me for the consultation.

She plays on the floor with building blocks and abacuses and broken dolls, clicking and clacking, drawing attention as any toddler would, whilst the sisterhood looks on imagining 'what ifs', feeling something heavy, dreaming something else and looking somewhat angry at me, forcing them to bear witness to the moving image of what they have come to abort. With the heaviest heart I have ever felt, I end the pregnancy with a single pill. To make such a decision when I already know the worth of human life through my daughters devastates me; I cry so many hot tears through chilly November, but with this sacrifice, I realise how desperate I am to regain control of my life.

As a woman, I have a choice; I at least have power and sovereignty over my body, and my body can't house another child, not now, not with him. So I play the little poppy seed haunting Eastern European music in a market square and then later bleed it out like a squashed plum onto the mattress. November's the month notorious for its full slaughterhouses that hold all that could not survive the winter. I spend a few weeks fever furious, in contorting agony, under wet sheets and nightmares until December swings open her steel doors and suddenly it seems too cold for snow.

When R realises I'm serious, he resists, threatening to destroy my things if I try to go. I've messed with his precious notion of famiglia, and as he loses control, I lose patience. It's messy at the end, violent even – a pattern I recognise from my parents' relationship – but I succeed in getting away. How do we endure the unendurable? We just do. Mostly.

'Attention please, you will not get out of here alive'.

*

When I was a child, I used to map out London on a broken BMX bike, which you'd never mistake for R's Suzuki but which served the same purpose: escape. I was only allowed to go so far, but every day I went further; once I went so far, I lost my way. I'd gone beyond my street, the shops beyond, the underground platform, the alleyway, across a park, over a roundabout and down an exit road thrilled when I realised I'd mounted a dual carriageway, no fear.

I ran with a little herd of wildlings and strays who met at random far from home and exchanged stories. There were home-less kids, kids whose home wasn't safe, runaways and refugees, gangs from various postcodes, and I joined them with my wide eyes. I wasn't just a tomboy, but also a hunter-gatherer, a ring-master and an explorer. I was gone all day, yet somehow, I wasn't killed. Years later, when I asked my mother why she let me roam from dusk until dawn outside when I was as young as ten years old, she replied 'I couldn't stop you!', a lesson R also had to learn.

When I visited Algeria in my teens, I took my love of wander-ing with me. It was humid indoors, where I was kept beside my female kinsfolk. I asked if I could go out walking just for some cool air and was told that women were not allowed out alone. Finally, on one occasion after much begging, I was given a male cousin, Rashid, as a guide; he took me to the top of a hill over the town and kissed me hard in the heat. I was fourteen and apart from an affectionate parental peck had never been kissed before. Being outside in Algeria felt dangerous after that; I had no rights, only the men did, the right to do whatever they wanted, including posing as carers to take advantage. If I'd told anyone in Algeria what Rashid had done, it would have just been my fault for going out, I was safer at home scrubbing floors and learning to cook boureka with my aunties for a future Husband.

Italy didn't feel so different after Algeria. I didn't know where I fit into the cityscape in either country where chastity rules and tradition had me chained to the kitchen stove. The men turned on bright lights to see me properly. I swapped one form of domineering and aggressive energy for another, as it was the only masculine love I knew. I was lucky, I got away from my father and R. My *lonerlust* saw me through.

The tiny Tintoretto skies in Italy are always close to my heart. Sometimes I feel I can dive in and under with a little splash, but safely swim back out again, to board my vessel, paddle the oars in my wish direction and reach another shore outside of the frame still breathing. No one gets out of life alive, but you can pull out of the rotunda of trauma alive, pass through little platforms with lessons to heal, wounds to lick, a mountain lion with her pride of cubs – there is no panic in this sacred medicine, from husk to bright wing, we transform, again and again; the liminal space between wakefulness and dreams –

'Attention please, you will get out of here alive'.

SEA CROSSINGS: TIME CIRCLES

Margaret Elphinstone

Waves race before the south-westerly. Ripples of white run along each crest as the sea shallows. Each wave curls white all along the bay, tips on itself and falls. When I listen to the waves, time isn't a straight line any more. The rhythm changes but never ceases. Swell, fall, crash, swirl. Moon, tide, weather and the beat of my own heart are all part of it, but the waves broke long before I came and they'll keep on breaking long after I've gone. When I'm by the sea I remember this.

I know perfectly well this planet is not only round and finite, but forensically mapped. Longitude has been computed; the mythical islands of the Atlantic are either colonised or deleted. I've crossed time zones and discovered the only reality that changes is my inner clock. And yet … out there where sea meets sky, something remains unfathomable. The sea journeys that punctuate my life don't stretch away into distant time like looking through the wrong end of a telescope. Instead they shift like beads in a kaleidoscope. I'm far enough along to start seeing the pattern. It's not linear; it's more a matter of colours changing in different lights.

Living on the island, we can only cross to the mainland when the sea lets us through. That winter we wait a month. I have my children to look after and an old couple to see to each day. I keep the fire in, put food on the table, walk the kids to school through wind and rain, and in the dark evenings, by the light of the Tilley lamp I write a book. All this within sound of the sea. Sometimes I lie on the cliff top, rain beating on my back, and feel the ground shake under me as each wave hits land. White water surges through the sound between the island and the mainland. Nothing could cross that sea. I want that month to last for ever: in a way it has.

Coming home from Mainland to Papa Stour, a blue and white speck breaks free of the island, appears and vanishes between each swell, grows, takes shape slowly, and at last we hear the *Venture* chugging over the sound of the waves. She slips alongside, John o Midsetter at the wheel under the slim shelter of the wheelhouse. Everything is heaved aboard: sacks of potatoes, bags of coal, boxes of shopping from Sandness stores, crates of chickens, haversacks, baskets and then children, lifted over the gunwale or jumping down between helping hands. And then us: Marianne, Vicki, me: young mothers standing behind the skipper, our offspring stowed in the cuddy under the wheelhouse, in our thick jerseys and hippy scarves, our long hair tangled by the wind. We cross the sea into a different life of our own choosing, bringing up kids on a small island. We think we're going to change the world.

We hit the swell as we leave the lee of Melby. Whitecaps flash in sunlight a few yards away; we steer clear, past Melby Holm into the smooth tide-race. The engine changes tune. The *Venture* slides east while it heads north. We pass Forwick Holm and – this is a calm enough day – between Maiden Stack and North Ness. The engine echoes between cliffs as guillemots circle indignantly above us. We enter Housa Voe. Warm land embraces us. The first house I see is our own, across the field from the jetty.

In that present tense my journey ends there.

Time folds over: swell, fall, crash, swirl. As I cross the sea from Lerwick to Torshavn, and Stóra Dímon and Litla Dímen take form out of the mist, time circles back to the first time I came here. Free to go anywhere, with a fresh new degree and not a clue what could hold me back, I arrived in Faroe with my sights set on Iceland. Back then – 1971 – I found a Faroese way of life that's long gone, but piercing my genuine nostalgia is the memory of the foetus ripped from the belly of a dying whale and the only time in my life I ever fainted outright, finding myself lying on the wet beach boulders surrounded by the legs of people bending over me. Our host had whisked us in his boat to the heart of the whale hunt as soon as the message came. I saw the killing, and the pilot whales flung ashore by the surging wave of their massed flight. I watched unwounded whales being slaughtered to stop them thrashing, and the rest left to die. I saw the men climb up ladders to measure each one. I saw the red waves break sluggishly on the beach among the dying animals.

That night I joined the whale dance at the top of the beach, a circle of humanity stamping out steps in the dark to the beat of their ballad, celebrating the defeat of cold and hunger for another winter. Each time I faced seawards I saw the shadowed corpses on the beach. It turned out I was pregnant too; a few weeks later I was sick all the way back to Copenhagen in the *Kronprinz Frederik*. So life circled, and Iceland receded beyond impassable waves for another twenty-one years, while I was in another place.

Time slipped by like the green tide surging through Papa Sound. Now – 1992 – the island is Vagur, and I'm looking at the pyramidical Faroe Islands to west and south, as I used to look at triangular Foula from Papa Stour; there were days when it looked barely a mile away, and other days when it was lost in weather. The sea carves out the Faroe Islands in sharp shapes that remind me strangely of the Arizona desert – maybe not so strange: the whole West of America was once under the sea. But here the imprint of the ice is dominant. The glaciers might have melted yesterday. The ghost of ice remains, a memory of an un-human world. Among rockfalls and waterfalls are little flowers – tormentil, eyebright, moss campion – that look fragile, but they've survived everything. They wouldn't be the way they are if it wasn't for rock and ice.

I'm on my own again, and the crossing to Iceland is open.

Norröna enters the strait between Eystoróy and Borðóy. The panorama of the northern islands is a map come alive – there's where I crossed from Leirvik to Klaksvik on Borðóy. There's Fuglóy where my tent blew down in a Force 9 gale and I found refuge, along with four Dutch tourists, in the pastor's house. There's Gjóv, with its lovely wooden hostel and prayer leaflets; there are the cliffs below Sandfelli which I climbed a week ago. The sea's getting rougher, but I watch until the islands disappear into the dusk.

On this crowded ferry I begin to wonder what this travelling is all about. I spend my last Faroese kröner on breakfast, and while I eat I talk to a geologist from Mainz. On deck, as Iceland is coming into view, he tells me about the rocks – what was done by volcanoes, and what was done by the glaciers. Seeing Iceland … watching the mountains and the cliffs and fjords acquiring depth, I hardly believe it's real. I fear there must be an anticlimax, but there isn't. The place is still there, waiting.

The bus heads west along dirt roads round Vatnajökull. There's a strip of green between the glacier and the sea: at least, green in places. We cross deserts of lava and cinders like the sea. The eruptions of 1362 and 1783 might have happened yesterday. There are extraordinary cliff formations, mountains rising out of nothing, strange islands that used not to be islands. It's seeing the land *actually being made*, just as the geologist had said. Nothing's static, just the timescale is so different we don't notice. Farms sit in their green islands of bright grass – called 'toon' just like in Scotland. There are pastures above – 'hagar' like 'hagi' in Shetland, and the rest is wilderness, never been touched. Everyone here lives under a volcano.

My idea of Iceland becomes inhabited by real people. I worked in Shetland Library long enough to read my way through the Icelandic sagas. I hitch-hike to the saga places, and people who give me lifts talk about things that are happening today, or maybe a thousand years ago. A lorry drops me at Bergðorshvoll, and a woman stops earthing up potatoes to see who I am. My Icelandic dictionary tells me what to say: "Is Njala Saga here?". She sticks her fork in the soil and takes me to see where Njal's house burned. She points out the path Flosi and the burners took from Thridyrningur, and where they hid before they attacked. All this in the present tense.

With Agnar and Hlif on Hunafjord, I feed calves, milk cows, and learn about modern haymaking and Icelandic byres. Hlif tells me about her ancestor, Aud the Deep-Minded, who landed at Dogverdernes – Breakfast-ness – and wisely began twelve hundred plus years of settlement with breakfast. Hlif takes me visiting, and teaches me to make skyr, and Agnar argues with me. We argue about Scottish Independence and how to make black pudding, about poetic metre and Cod Wars, about imperialism, standing armies and language policing. Agnar makes me listen to the sagas in Old Norse. Agnar died in 2024 while I was writing this, so here and now I can celebrate the part he played in anything I ever learned about Iceland.

Gudrid took me to Greenland. I found her at the primary school in Stykkishólmur on Snaefellsnes. One could stay very cheaply in rural primary schools in Iceland during the summer holidays. I was alone, and round me on the classroom walls were the children's paintings from last year's project. I recognised the story, and its heroine, from *Greenland Saga* and *Eirik's Saga*. As I circled the room, cradling my mug of coffee, I started to wonder who Gudrid really was. What was it like to be a woman in her world? To live inside her skin? I decided to follow her to Vinland

and back, to find out.

Time curls over and swirls round me. I sit where Gudrid once sat, on the doorstep of Brattahlið, Eirik the Red's house in Greenland. I'm making notes for Gudrid's story as I go, in a tattered exercise book stained with coffee rings and sea. I sketch things I see, and because I have no way of colouring in, I write notes on them – 'sea turquoise close to, grey further off.' I draw the icebergs that dot the fjord and, beyond, the grey mountain Ilerfissalik, which Gudrid would have known as Burfjeld, with its gleaming glaciers.

I become Gudrid, sitting on the doorstep of Brattahlið. The sea could have been exactly these colours on this same July afternoon a thousand years ago. Gudrid is scraping a fresh sheepskin to soften it. The part of me which is not Gudrid is writing in a notebook, but I know what it's like to scrape a sheepskin; Helen taught me when I was her home help on Papa Stour. As she sits on the doorstep, the Gudrid who is partly me watches Thorstein Eiriksson riding past, and listens to the clatter of his pony's hooves on the shore path. The rider in July 1995 is a young Greenlander who canters by on his pony right in the middle of my notes.

When Gudrid lived at Narsarsuaq it was called Stokkanes from the trees which grew there. Narsarsuaq has its own museum; the Danish curator takes me in his boat around the fjord Tunulliarfik, which Gudrid knew as Eiriksfjord. We visit Viking farms, just as Gudrid did, right along the fjord. Most of the farms are marked on the map, but none has been excavated. We scrunch ashore amidst wavelets on grey beaches below wizened birch trees and juniper, always close enough to a burn for the people in the farms to have heard it chattering on still nights. On the thin soil of the tundra every settlement is excellently sited and follows the same pattern: the long house, the byre, the barn, the store sheds, the boathouse and the milking ring. As we cross and re-cross the shimmering fjord I'm reminded that, on days when the sea lets you through, no shore is remote. Sometimes neighbours are consolingly near, and there are long months when they might as well be as far off as the moon.

I follow Gudrid to West Greenland. At Qaqortoq it's raining and I long to be indoors. The receptionist at the Seamen's Mission lets me lay out my sleeping bag in the laundry for quarter the price of a room. I drape my soggy tent and flysheet discreetly behind racks of bleach-white sheets. During the day I eat and write in the canteen looking over the fjord to Akia. A young man comes from the kitchen with my coffee, "In the kitchen they say I must ask you: is it your diary you write here every day, or do you write a book?"

The coastal ferry to Nuuk takes me by an ancient route into modern Greenland. Gudrid never met any Inuit people; in her time they never reached the Norse settlements. On the ferry we eat together round the table in the crowded cabin. At least half the passengers are children. We have no common language, but I understand: 'Try this,' 'a little of this,' 'give her some of that.' Someone spikes a forkful of what I think is seal meat from the brimming pan and offers it to me. I cannot empty my plate without its being filled at once. The trick, the opposite of what I was taught to do, is to stop eating. These families live scattered up and down the coast; in winter they don't see each other, but now everyone who can is going visiting.

'The water,' says Gudrid, 'was calm and black, and in the distance we could see mountains like dogs' teeth, and to our north the ice desert that covers the heart of the Green Land. When we came out west of Greenland the sea was benign: there was nothing but a great openness, the silvery light of the north, and icebergs as white as froth on cream. That's how I remember those seas most often now: the distance and the vast light.'

I pause, wondering whether to put quotation marks round the paragraph I've just written. Are those Gudrid's words, or mine? My memory is clear: that is exactly what I saw. But my Nuuk is very unlike her Sandnes. It's nearly midnight when I leave the warm lights of the ferry and walk into town. The prowling dogs and groups of men make me nervous. It's hard to remember how that felt, two days later when I'm having coffee and cake on the top floor of a brutalist tower block, with a young Greenlandic couple. Ila speaks English, and suddenly Nuuk, seen from the inside, becomes kindly and welcoming.

Gudrid had the hardest time of her life in this fjord. I go to the Nuuk museum, and see the monument, or is it an exhibition – the distinction makes me uneasy – dedicated to the Inuit group who starved to death in a cave more than five hundred years ago. Six women, a small boy, and a baby. Why, I wonder, where I come from, do people feel they are so entitled to survive, when most peoples, at most times, have lived much closer to death than we wish to believe? The Norse faded out of Greenland six hundred years ago, and now – 1995 – they say the ice is melting away too. I walked up the Narsarsuaq valley to the foot of the ice cap and laid my bare palms against it. Strangely, the wind off the ice brings warmth to the valley, owing to a particular kind of turbulence. Or it did back then, when I was there, and when Gudrid was there. It'll be different now.

Gudrid gave birth in a hut in Vinland, with no one to help her but a clutch of fortune-seeking men on the make. When she travelled to Rome did she cross Europe on a mule, or did she sail in an open boat along the Atlantic seaboard? I've seen Europe spread out like a map below me. Gudrid never saw a map in her life. She travelled to the ends of her world, and to its centre. In this I couldn't follow her, because my world has no ends and no centre. Labrador, Quebec, Newfoundland, New England … if I did reach Vinland

I was not exactly in it. I crossed the same seas as Gudrid, not in a Norse Knar ship but on modern ferries. Over the open Atlantic I mostly had to fly. I followed Gudrid from Glaumbaer on the north coast of Iceland to Rome, and I parted with her on the shores of Lake Bracciano, just as the monk Agnar does in my novel. But, as the sagas say so pithily, Gudrid is now out of this story.

The waves break whether there is anyone left to listen to them or not. Swell, fall, crash, swirl. The sea is my broad highway into the past, and now another boat, *MV Halton,* takes me to islands where people once lived, and to skerries where no human community could survive.

I discover *Halton* and her skipper Bob in Stromness – it's a new century now – when I'm seeking ways to get to lighthouses on uninhabited islands. Any boat will do, I think, but I'm wrong: *Halton* will be forever dear to me. *Halton* is a nine-metre Danish seine netter, traditionally built with oak carved planks on oak ribs, now converted to a dive boat, also able to carry disparate groups of people in her eight two-berth cabins. Her cosy deck house is both galley and viewing lounge; there's space in the wheelhouse for enthusiastic passengers, except at tense moments like navigating the Sound of Harris, when we supernumeraries have to stay out and keep quiet. I voyage with *Halton* and the Sule Skerry bird ringers for two seasons. The lighthouse on Sule Skerry enters my novel. On Sule Skerry we camp among puffins who mutter in their burrows under my tent throughout the summer nights. I watch fledged pufflings stumble towards the sea. Orcas circle the island hunting seals. Peering over the side of the inflatable, I see a basking shark just below. Humans are only summer migrants here. But it's the storm petrels who take over my book. I extricate petrels from mist nets, put them in bags, take them to be weighed and measured, and then release them. Storm petrels are light as air, softly frail, smoky-smelling, fitting in my cupped hands. Prisoner of gravity that I am, when I toss them away I always feel they'll fall; each time their take off is a little miracle as they sail upward into free air.

With *Halton* I voyage into a world without people: to the gannet colony on Sule Stack, in the inflatable through the sea-tunnels under Sula Sgeir, to the gigantic sea stacks beyond St Kilda. Most islands have a human past too. From the Neolithic roundhouses on St Kilda to the 1895 lighthouse on Sule Skerry, *Halton* takes me to stories which people have written on the land. On a day of absurd calm I lean from the inflatable and touch Duislic skerry at the foot of Cape Wrath, and I wonder who else once stood on this rock just for the hell of it. I kneel in the chapel on North Rona, now far from any inhabited island. I rest my notebook on a round stone and write down the place as close as I can get. I wait for the tide to fall round Shivinish where the people fled from the floods that tore the Monach islands apart four hundred years ago. I find a glass trawler float in a sand dune; it's thirty years since I last found one of those.

Halton takes me into my own present, with a cargo of musicians who play the Northern Isles of Orkney for a festival season. A different village hall every night, always cakes and ale, always the same concert. The tunes play themselves into my bones. Distance changes its meaning; we cross from Sanday to Eday, from Eday to Westray and Papa Westray. The islands thread together in a way I've never known. We come north past the Calf of Eday towards the evening sun. I sit in my favourite spot on the Samson post listening to the fiddles playing on the deck behind me. I sight pilot whales. The music stops. The whales roil around off the Calf. Some break away to swim alongside. The music starts again to keep them company. Such is magic.

Swell, fall, crash, swirl. Time circles – it's 2023 – and my own journey is still under way. For forty years I've wanted to sail from

Galloway, where I live, to the Isle of Man. Now, with the tiller under my hand, the sea reminds me how to steer, and I still know how to listen. Suddenly I'm no longer older and stiffer and no use with the foresails. Here at the tiller, I just am, like always.

The threads between Galloway and the Isle of Man run from the layers of rock that connect them to the first skin boats that crossed this sea; from the heyday of eighteenth-century smuggling to the opulence of Victorian steamers. From the shores of Galloway I see the Isle of Man as I used to see Foula from Papa Stour: close enough to see depth as well as outline on a summer day, then vanishing into cloud for weeks on end. But without a boat the other island is just an outline on the horizon which exists only in its own isolation, and sometimes not even that.

The tide changes in our favour as we pass the Mull. All I can hear is wind and sea. Dolphins leap beside us and dive under our bow. We're sailing on a broad reach, with all the time in the world to look about, and a well-mannered, beautifully-crafted boat to make this crossing. *Barbican* is a Bermudan cutter, built of mahogany and Canadian Rock Ash. The Mull of Galloway is fading into distance; the white speck of the lighthouse is almost gone.

Ruth, Cathy and I have travelled a long way since we met in Shetland fifty years ago. I can't count how often we've crossed the sea, or walked the hills into new country. At first there were no children, then there were always children, and now the children are living their own lives somewhere else. Each journey is distinct, yet they are all one. Cathy's brother, our skipper, made this crossing possible because my friends knew I needed to make it.

The Mull of Galloway lets go and slides northwards into the mist. There is no land anywhere, only choppy waves telling of tides swirling round coasts not far away. At last we see a faint grey line that could be a cloud, but isn't. The Isle of Man, as I know it from Galloway, has changed shape. I keep my sights on the hill just west of Peel, and steer towards it. The coast of Jurby gathers colour and dimension. The waves settle. As the western peninsula, with Peel huddled under its arm, comes closer, I recognise places on the port shore. I worked on the Isle of Man for a semester. It's accessible any day by plane from Glasgow, or on the huge car ferry from Heysham. I've driven Isle of Man roads, bought its groceries, walked through streets full of international banks, made friends here and I wrote a book while I was at it. So much for misty horizons.

The waves broke along these northern shores long before I came and they'll keep breaking long after I'm gone. Swell, fall, crash, swirl. I see a blue-green island. It looks like it's floating just across the strait. Cousin John and I sit by the gunwale, one on each side. We hold tight. I've never crossed the sea in an open boat before. My parents sit between us. The gap widens between our boat and the shore we've left behind. The boat rocks in the swell. The outboard chugs merrily. Waves slap the bow. The sea is so close I can touch it. I lick my hand. It tastes salt. The island draws near. I see hayfields, a village and a grey church just to the north. I already know who made that church. I know which sea he crossed and why he came. My mother told me the story last night. Columba came to Iona in 563 and now it's 1956. He came with his monks in a skin boat all the way from Ireland to bring faith and hope to the islands. Iona was a special island before Columba came, said my mother, "then he made it more special, and now it always will be."

We come alongside a sloping jetty. The boatman helps me stand on the gunwale and I jump. I land on a different island. I have crossed the sea and what was previously *there* is now *here*.

This is it.

THE CONTRIBUTORS

ESA ALDEGHERI is a Scottish-Italian writer, scholar and educator. She is the author of *Free to Go – across the world on a motorbike* (John Murray, 2022), a travel book exploring the limits of freedom and non-freedom, motorbike journeys, motherhood and more. Her other writing has been variously anthologised, has featured on BBC Radio 4's *Book of the Week* and has been published by Granta, Gutter and others. Esa is a Leverhulme EC Fellow at the University of Glasgow, researching how unequal narratives and bordering of refugee journeys affect community integration. She also loves sea swimming, tree climbing and map reading.

ROXANI KRYSTALLI is an academic at the University of St Andrews, where her research and teaching focus on feminist peace and conflict studies, as well as on the politics of nature and place. A key question animating Roxani's writing and work is how people imagine and enact worlds in the wake of loss. Her first book, *Good Victims*, was published in 2024. Roxani is currently co-leading a research project on the politics of love and care. She is from Greece and lives in Scotland.

LEENA RUSTOM NAMMARI is a Palestinian artist living in Scotland. She has exhibited widely within Scotland, Europe, China, Australia and Palestine, as part of group and solo exhibitions. She has worked as a printmaking technician, studio manager/co-ordinator, master printer and printmaking educator at Edinburgh

Printmakers Workshop, and as a freelance art educator with various organisations, including Scottish National Galleries and the RSA. She worked as a nurse for many years prior to her undergraduate in Fine Art Printmaking in 2000, and completed her MFA in 2018. She embarked on a practice-based PhD at DJCAD in 2022.

LINDA CRACKNELL is a writer of fiction and narrative non-fiction who also writes for radio. Her writing is inspired by place and memory. As well as a subject in itself, walking and motion are essential to her creative process. She has had two fiction books published, *Call of the Undertow* (2013) and *The Other Side of Stone* (2022). Her non-fiction books include essay collection *Writing Landscape: Taking Note, Making Notes* (2023); *Doubling Back: Paths trodden in memory* (2024) and *Sea Marked: Throwing a Line to the Mother Ship* (forthcoming). She lives in Highland Perthshire.

AMANDA THOMSON is a Scottish visual artist and writer who lives and works in Strathspey and Glasgow. Her essays have appeared in several anthologies and she has written and read her essays for BBC Radio 3 and 4. Her first book, *A Scots Dictionary of Nature,* was published by Saraband, and *Belonging: Natural Identities of Place, Identity and Home* (Canongate Books) was shortlisted for the Wainwright Prize for Nature Writing in 2023. She has exhibited her artwork nationally and internationally, with her film essay, *Boundary Layers*, being part of Scotland's collateral exhibition at the Venice Architecture Biennale in 2023.

SARAH THOMAS is an interdisciplinary artist, writer and traveller. A PhD in Interdisciplinary Studies from the University of Glasgow resulted in her debut *The Raven's Nest* (Atlantic Books, 2022), an ecological memoir set in Iceland, which was longlisted for the inaugural Nan Shepherd Prize and shortlisted for the Fitzcarraldo Essay Prize. She has taught creative writing for Arvon Foundation and various universities. Shaped by an upbringing in Kenya and a half decade in Iceland, she can currently be found tramping the intertidal zone of south-west Scotland. 'Stay At Home' is an extract from a book in progress.

LEONIE CHARLTON lives in Glen Lonan, Argyll, with her family and animals. Publications include her award-winning poetry pamphlet *Ten Minutes of Weather Away* published by Cinnamon Press in 2021, and her travel memoir *Marram*, published by Sandstone Press in 2020. *Marram* was Waterstones' April 2022 Scottish Book of the Month. Leonie completed her MLitt at Stirling University in 2016, and is currently doing a creative writing practice-based PhD with the University of Highlands and Islands looking at Scotland's deer debate. She is fascinated by our emotional, cultural, and environmental connection with place and the more-than-human world. www.leoniecharlton.co.uk

DR CLAIRE ASKEW's books include the creative writing guide *Novelista* (John Murray, 2020), the multi-award-winning novel *All The Hidden Truths* (Hodder & Stoughton, 2018) and the poetry collections *This changes things* (2016) and *How To Burn A Woman* (2021), both from Bloodaxe Books. Claire has worked as a Scottish Book Trust Reading Champion, a Jessie Kesson Fellow, and as the University of Edinburgh's Writer in Residence. She lives in Cumbria.

ANNA FLEMING is a writer from mid-Wales and Scotland. An active traveller and climber, she collects stories of people, mountains and nature from around the world. Her memoir, *Time on Rock* (Canongate 2022) was shortlisted for the Wainwright Prize and

Boardman-Tasker Award. Her PhD with the University of Leeds examined Wordsworth's creativity and Cumbrian communities. When at home, she can be found in Edinburgh.

LEE CRAIGIE was Scotland's Active Nation Commissioner and founder of female-led not-for-profit The Adventure Syndicate. A trained outdoor instructor and child therapist, Lee then became the British Mountain Bike Champion in 2013 and represented Scotland at the 2014 Commonwealth Games. She has told stories of inspiring adventure through her award-winning film *Divided* and in her latest book, which won the Vicki Orvice Women's prize for sports writing, *Other Ways to Win*. She has contributed to other literary anthologies including *Imagine a World* and *Waymaking*. Lee presented the popular BBC Scotland radio series *Lifecycle* and has delivered a TedX talk to wide acclaim. She is an Honorary Fellow of the Royal Scottish Geographical Society and lives in the Highlands of Scotland.

MARJORIE LOTFI is the author of *The Wrong Person to Ask* (Bloodaxe Books, 2023), winner of the inaugural James Berry Prize and a Poetry Book Society Special Commendation. She co-authored *The World May Be the Same* (Stewed Rhubarb Press, 2023), a collection of poetry about the experiences of people of colour living in Scotland, with the writer Hannah Lavery. Her poetry has won awards and been published widely, most recently on London's Poems on the Underground. She is currently working on a memoir about her childhood in revolutionary Iran and Ohio.

ALICE TARBUCK is an award-winning poet and writer. Her debut non-fiction book, *A Spell in the Wild: a year (and six centuries) of Magic*, is published by Hodder & Stoughton. With Claire Askew, she is the co-editor of *The Modern Craft*, published by Watkins.

She is a previous winner of the Scottish Book Trust New Writer's Award for poetry, and recipient of their award for programming. She has taught Creative Writing at the Universities of Dundee and York, and is a Lead Reader for *Open Book*. Alice is currently Writer in Residence on the AHRC funded Print Matters project at the University of York.

JEMMA NEVILLE is an author, journalist and explorer living in rural East Lothian. Her travel writing has been published in the *Guardian*, The National Trust for Scotland magazine and *Preferred Travel* magazine. Jemma's nonfiction book, *Constitution Street*, is the story of a daily walk along one street in Edinburgh and the interconnecting lives of the people she met. She won The Creative Edinburgh Award, has twice been highly commended in The Anne Brown Essay Prize and was a finalist in the *Guardian's* International Development Journalism Award.

KERRI NÍ DOCHARTAIGH is a mother, writer, holder and grower. She has written for the *Guardian*, *BBC, RTE, Irish Times* and others. She mentors and teaches worldwide. Her work currently explores ideas of 'one-amotherness', interconnectedness and ecologies of care. Her first book, *Thin Places,* for which she won the 2022 Butler Literary Award and was highly commended in the 2021 Wainwright Prize for Nature Writing, was published by Canongate in spring 2021. *Cacophony of Bone* was published by Canongate in May 2023 and was longlisted for the Wainwright Prize for Nature Writing in the same year. She lives in the west of Ireland with her family.

ROSEANNE WATT is a writer, filmmaker and musician from Shetland. Her dual-language debut collection, *Moder Dy*, was published by Polygon in May 2019, after receiving the prestigious Edwin Morgan Poetry Award for Scottish poets under thirty. *Moder Dy* subsequently received both an Eric Gregory and Somerset Maugham Award in 2020, and was named joint winner of the Highland Book Prize 2019. In 2019, Roseanne completed a funded doctorate from the University of Stirling in the disciplines of creative writing and filmmaking. She is currently poetry editor for the online literary journal *The Island Review*.

ALISON PHIPPS is UNESCO Chair for Refugee Integration through Education, Languages and Arts at the University of Glasgow. A poet and regular columnist in *The National*, her first solo anthology, *Through Wood*, was published in 2008, and her collection with Tawona Sitholé, *The Warriors Who Do Not Fight*, in 2018 (both with Wild Goose). In 2024, she published *Keep Telling of Gaza* with Khawla Badwan (Sídhe Press). She has two more poetry anthologies forthcoming with Wild Goose in 2025.

JANETTE AYACHI is a Scottish-Algerian poet. She is a regular on BBC arts programmes & collaborates with artists & performs at festivals internationally. Her first poetry book *Hand Over Mouth Music* (Pavilion, Liverpool University Press) won the Saltire Poetry Book of the Year Literary Award 2019 & her poetry, prose & essays have been published & translated into a broad range of newspapers, magazines & anthologies. Her book *QuickFire, Slow Burning* (Pavilion, LUP) was Longlisted for The Laurel Prize 2024. She is now writing her travel memoir *Lonerlust* & her debut fiction novel *Of Sweet Figs and Forget-Me-Nots*.

MARGARET ELPHINSTONE has written nine historical novels, including *The Gathering Night, Voyageurs* and the award-winning *Sea Road,* that span many lands and centuries with characters inhabiting liminal locations in times of disruption. More recently her poetry and essays, infused with urgency and foreboding, have displayed passionate awareness of the natural world's fragility. These concerns inspired her novella, *Lost People*. Shortlisted for the 2024 Saltire award, it offers hope and redemption in a time of war and desolation. She has worked as an organic gardener and an academic and is Emerita Professor of writing at Strathclyde University. She lives in Galloway.

ACKNOWLEDGEMENTS

Thank you to all the women whose stories have given me shelter and nourishment along the way, reaching across time and lands and languages. Without them, this book would never have begun.

Before I set out into the wide world, I was lucky enough to grow up surrounded by a family whose love and stories brought courage and wonder. Grazie, thank you, to Rita, Giovanni, Lorenzo, Jack and Jenny, Emilio, Kitty and George.

The paths I have travelled have been brightened by the enthusiasm and encouragement of many shining friends, there to celebrate the good times and bring consolation in seasons of darkness. Thank you, all of you.

To the people who have shown me that not all those who travel are equal, and that travel is not equal for all – colleagues in Palestine, Lebanon, Torino, Palermo, Glasgow and Edinburgh – thank you for opening up new horizons of questions.

To my wonderful Compañero whose love has been a steadfast star in all our years of adventuring: grazie, Querido. Sempre.

To my parents-in-love: infinite gratitude for your constant warmth and welcome. You are wonderful.

To my children: grazie, ragazzi, per tutto! Siete fantastici.

Thank you to Rosie and Sara at Saraband, for the intuition and care you have shown in accompanying *There She Goes* from proposal to actual book. I am also grateful to Creative Scotland for the funding which helped this book on its way.

Many thanks to Jenny Brown, Queen of Agents, for your wisdom and kindness and the joy you bring to the business of making books happen.

ACKNOWLEDGEMENTS

And a special thank you to the contributors of *There She Goes*, for responding to my invitation, for trusting that this adventure would work out, and for sharing your words with the world in these pages.

EDITORIAL NOTE

Non-English languages have not been italicised within this book, at the request of the contributors and editor, to avoid any risk of appearing to exoticise or other any language included here, or to perpetuate any hierarchy of any one language over another. Spellings, accents and transliteration in non-English languages are given as each contributor has provided their text, which may include informal usages and dialects.